W9-APG-438

THIS MEANS WAR

A STRATEGIC PRAYER JOURNAL

By ALEX KENDRICK and STEPHEN KENDRICK

with TROY SCHMIDT

B&H
PUBLISHING GROUP
Nashville, Tennessee

Copyright © 2015 Kendrick Brothers, LLC
All rights reserved.

Written by Stephen Kendrick and Alex Kendrick, with Troy Schmidt

Printed in the United States of America

978-1-4336-8870-6

Published by B&H Publishing Group, Nashville, Tennessee
BHPublishingGroup.com

Dewey Decimal Classification: J248.3

Subject Heading: PRAYER / SPIRITUAL WARFARE / CHRISTIAN LIFE

Unless otherwise noted, all Scripture quotations are taken from
the Holman Christian Standard Bible®, Copyright © 1999, 2000,
2002, 2003, 2009 by Holman Bible Publishers.

1 2 3 4 5 6 • 19 18 17 16 15

CONTENTS

WELCOME TO WAR 1

BOOT CAMP 29

THE ARSENAL 52

BASIC TRAINING................................80

ADVANCED TRAINING.........................130

SNIPER SCHOOL................................156

THE WAR ROOM JOURNAL....................205

WELCOME TO WAR

WELCOME TO WAR

CHAPTER 1
REPORTING FOR DUTY

The LORD advances like a warrior; He stirs up His zeal like a soldier. He shouts, He roars aloud, He prevails over His enemies.
—Isaiah 42:13

Most people, if asked, say they pray.

Most people, if asked what area of their spiritual life lacks the greatest, say prayer.

So people are praying yet they say they aren't praying well. What's wrong?

Using 140 characters or less, write your current status (yes, count spaces).

_____

_____

_____

_____

Short, sweet, to the point. What you're doing . . . how you're feeling . . . where you are . . .

This is how we communicate with the world these days—in posts, tweets, quick pictures, and emoticons. Prayer for many people is like tossing a tweet to God.

We don't pray, we give God our status updates.

Is that anyway to talk to the *COMMANDER IN CHIEF* of the world?

You're not just talking to a friend (though God is your friend).

You're not just talking to your parents (though God is your Father).

You're not just talking to your boss (though God is King).

You're talking to a God who made and rules over the universe.

The God who loves you.

And since God loves you, He wants to hear from you.

But God doesn't just want status updates.

He wants to hear your heart.

He wants to hear your passion.

He wants to hear about your pain.

He wants to hear your confessions.

He wants you to listen.

He wants you to know Him.

He wants you to grow in faith and worship.

He can't do that in 45 seconds and 140 characters or less. It takes time, emotion, and surrendering yourself before *THE GOD OF THE UNIVERSE*.

DESCRIBE YOUR PRAYER TIME with God.

_____

_____

_____

_____

_____

_____

How can it be better?

_____

_____

_____

_____

_____

_____

_____

Over the course of this book, we're going to go through training, understanding what prayer is all about. Your Commander in Chief is calling you to war, but first He needs to spend some time with you. It's day one, and you are reporting for duty. God has great things planned for you. If you will stick with this journal to the end, your life will be radically changed for the better. Fasten your seatbelt!

GO TO WAR

Can you spend 15 minutes with God and God alone right now? Just talk to Him. Don't follow any pattern or agenda. Just talk.

What was that like?

_____

_____

_____

_____

Don't worry. It should only get better from here!

WELCOME TO WAR

CHAPTER 2
WARRIORS

Then the Angel of the Lord appeared to him and said: "The Lord is with you, mighty warrior."—Judges 6:12

Soldiers fight. They struggle.

They go up against flesh and blood in hand-to-hand combat.

The goal in battle is to conquer your opponent.

Both sides want to win, and one side will only win when the other side is defeated.

This journal is preparing you, that warrior, for that battle.

You see, there's a war going on. Many of us think that battle is up to God and His angels to deal with and we're just helpless pawns in the whole deal.

We're not. We're warriors too. We are supposed to fight right in the middle of this battle. We can! But we must learn to battle courageously and effectively!

Why is prayer like battle?

_____

_____

_____

_____

_____

_____

_____

_____

First of all, when we pray, we get to talk to the *COMMANDER IN CHIEF* and tell Him how we feel, what we need, and ask Him what He wants us to do.

Tell a Private in today's army he can call the President of the United States any time he wants and he'll laugh at you. Presidents may not talk to low-ranking soldiers, but our God does.

Second of all, when we pray, we prepare our HEARTS for what's to come and protect ourselves for what's coming at us.

Do we need more ammunition? More assistance? More information? More patience? More faith? Prayer is preparation for the battle and protection during the battle.

Third, when we pray, we hear from our Commander in Chief and *FOLLOW HIS ORDERS*.

We align our WILL to God's. It's not about what we want, but what God wants.

Once you talk to the Commander, receive your orders, and follow them by aligning your will to His, God joins you in this battle. You are not alone!

How do you feel knowing God is with you?

_____

_____

_____

_____

If God is with you, how does that help you?

_____

_____

_____

_____

_____

How do you like the idea of becoming a warrior?

_____

_____

_____

_____

GO TO WAR

Name one battle that is going on in the world or in your life. Pray imagining another war, an unseen battle going on around that situation. Your prayers are taking aim at the battle. What are you aiming at? Fire away!

_____

_____

_____

_____

WELCOME TO WAR

CHAPTER 3
THE ENEMY

Be serious! Be alert! Your adversary the Devil is prowling around like a roaring lion, looking for anyone he can devour.
—*1 Peter 5:8*

In war, you have to know your enemy.

The enemy weakens the opposition by cutting off communication and separating the soldiers from their commander. Without guidance, the soldiers become confused and things fall apart.

Your enemy during prayer is Satan. His names indicate his motivations.

SATAN means "adversary," someone who opposes good and righteousness.

DEVIL means "accuser," someone who makes you feel guilty, shameful.

LUCIFER means "light," someone who disguises himself as something good, but tricks you into something bad.

The ENEMY will try to DISTRACT you, DECEIVE you, and DIVIDE you from a relationship with God. He will do anything he can to keep you out of the fight.

DISTRACTIONS could be things like too much entertainment, or wrong relationships. They can even be good things that pull you away from God's priorities. They pretend to be more important than they are.

His DECEPTIONS might include believing a lie about yourself or doubting whether God's Word is true.

And if he can DIVIDE you from God, or your family, or the church, then he can get an advantage in the fight by weakening you.

In the end, the Enemy wants you to stop talking to the Commander in Chief.

That way . . .

- You'll be lost and confused.

- You'll be unprepared and hurt.

- You'll follow the wrong orders and mess up.

- You'll grow dissatisfied with God and look for a different path.

- You'll distance yourself thinking God doesn't love you or He doesn't care.

- You'll stay out of the fight and give up.

PRETTY DEVIOUS PLAN, HUH?

The Enemy wants you to stop talking to the Commander in Chief. Don't let him win!

ANALYZE Satan's strategy to stop you from praying. How does he do that in your life?

_____

_____

_____

_____

_____

_____

_____

What are things that DISTRACT you?

_____

_____

_____

_____

_____

What are things that DECEIVE you?

_____

_____

_____

_____

What are things that DIVIDE you (from church, family, and God)?

_____

_____

_____

_____

_____

GO TO WAR

Pray that God will show you the ways Satan keeps you from prayer. Pray against all the distractions, deceptions, and divisions invading your life.

WELCOME TO WAR

CHAPTER 4
THE BATTLE PLAN

"For I know the plans I have for you"—this is the Lord's declaration—"plans for your welfare, not for disaster, to give you a future and a hope."—Jeremiah 29:11

How do you know the battle plan? Sending short transmissions to headquarters doesn't get the job done.

God wants you to FIGHT the problems that you see around you with prayer and nonstop communication with God.

This will take time, but it will be time well spent. Look what you will experience according to Jeremiah 29:11 when you discover that battle plan.

WELFARE—plans that benefit you and those around you.

TRIUMPH (not disaster)—plans that succeed and give glory to God.

FUTURE—plans that have long-reaching effects starting now and into eternity.

HOPE—plans that give you security and something to look forward to.

God has plans for you. Excellent plans.

The Commander in Chief has specific marching orders for you.

To know those plans, you must . . .

Draw near to God and He will draw near to you.
—James 4:8

You have to get close to God. God speaks through His Word and His Spirit, but He sometimes speaks in whispers (1 Kings 19:12), and you can't hear whispers unless you are close to the source.

"If you seek Me, you will find Me, if you seek Me with all your heart."—Jeremiah 29:13

You have to pursue God to hear the plans. God promises you will find Him if you seek Him. If you don't seek Him, you won't find Him.

Put an X on this scale to describe your relationship with God.

NEAR---**FAR**

What do you need to do to get closer to God?

_____

_____

_____

_____

_____

What does God need to do to get closer to you?

_____

_____

_____

(Answer: nothing. He doesn't move away. We do.)

In what areas of your life do you want to hear God's plans? Circle them.

School/college

Career

Future spouse

Dating/relationships

Parents

Friends

Other: _____

Remember, God wants to give you welfare, triumph, a future, and hope in all these areas. If you hear anything else besides these things (loss, despair, hopelessness), they are words from the Enemy.

What will your life look like if you drew closer to God?

_____

_____

_____

_____

_____

_____

GO TO WAR

Pray imagining yourself close to God, at His feet, in His arms. Read His Word and listen as He whispers His plans for you. Hear those plans and obey.

WELCOME TO WAR

CHAPTER 5
A GOOD SOLDIER

"His master said to him, 'Well done, good and faithful slave! You were faithful over a few things; I will put you in charge of many things. Share your master's joy!'"—Matthew 25:21

What are the qualities of a good soldier in battle?

_____

_____

_____

_____

_____

_____

Which of those qualities signify your prayer life? PUT A STAR next to them.

- A good soldier fights for what is good.

- A good soldier never leaves his post.

- A good soldier never associates with the enemy.

- A good soldier never gives up no matter what happens around him.

- A good soldier listens to his Commander in Chief.

- A good soldier is loyal.

- A good soldier sacrifices himself for others.

- A good soldier knows what he needs to do and does it.

The Bible is filled with soldiers, men and women who engaged in battle either on the front lines in hand-to-hand combat or as a commander.

ABRAHAM fought an alliance of kings to save his nephew Lot (Genesis 14).

MOSES raised his arms so the soldiers would win a battle (Exodus 17).

DEBORAH, a prophetess, communicated the battle plans to the commanders (Judges 4).

GIDEON reduced the size of his army to give God more glory (Judges 7).

DAVID, small in stature but large in faith, took on Goliath (1 Samuel 17).

Every person in the Bible, in some way, went to war, from kings to prophets to apostles. They fought for what was right. They faced opposition, kept their faith, and saw victory.

It's not much different today.

You are a soldier in a fight. You may not have a sword in your hand, but you have the Word of God. You may not have blood on your shirt, but you have sweat, from hours of strenuous communication with God.

In the end, when the battle is done and you enter the Promised Land, what words do you want your Commander in Chief to say to you?

_____

_____

_____

_____

_____

_____

_____

_____

What accolade on earth would compare to hearing God say that to you?

_____

_____

_____

_____

_____

_____

Become that kind of prayer warrior so that one day, when you cross that threshold into eternity, you will hear your Commander in Chief say to you, *"Well done, good and faithful soldier"* (Matthew 25:23).

GO TO WAR

Pray as a good and faithful soldier right now. What does a good soldier pray for? How does a faithful soldier pray?

WELCOME TO WAR

CHAPTER 6
FIGHTING FOR GOD'S KIND OF PEACE

"Don't assume that I came to bring peace on the earth. I did not come to bring peace, but a sword."—Matthew 10:34

Good soldiers fight for the right kind of peace.

Even Jesus realized that entering enemy territory would create casualties. In Matthew 10:35–36, Jesus outlined those victims.

". . . a man against his father,
   a daughter against her mother,
      a daughter-in-law against her mother-in-law;
         and a man's enemies will be
            the members of his household."

When you dedicate yourself to Jesus Christ, not every relationship in your life will be thrilled. Some separate from you because you've joined God's army. In some countries, embracing Christ may mean being rejected by your family.

Jesus told His followers to expect broken relationships when you go to war.

Jesus wanted to make sure that those going to battle were willing to sacrifice it all for Him. No other relationship can stand in the way of a person's dedication to the Commander, Jesus Christ. Not friends. Not family.

Jesus' goal is not to destroy those relationships. He wants to heal them. He wants the fighting to stop between those factions. But it must be on His terms. Compromising His truth doesn't bring His kind of peace, but praying for them and loving them the way Jesus loved us can bring life change to them, and therefore lead to real peace.

So the good soldier wonders, *I've dedicated myself to the Commander in Chief and yet I'm seeing all this strife still. My friends and family think I'm crazy. I thought life would get easier.*

Fighting for God only magnifies the battle. The need for peace increases. And what ultimately leads to peace?

Surrender. Someone always has to surrender. When we surrender to the Lord and His ways, He can work in ways we cannot.

Jesus went to the cross and died so we can have peace with God. His stance caused division between family and friends and yet His sacrifice unified God and man.

Are you glad Jesus fought for peace between you and God?

YES   **NO**

Is fighting for peace a contradiction? Why or why not?

_____

_____

_____

_____

_____

_____

_____

_____

A person with cancer fights for health.

A pastor fights for truth.

A policeman fights for justice.

You fight for peace in a difficult situation by praying for a resolution.

You fight for peace between people and God by praying for reconciliation.

You fight for peace in yourself by praying for realization.

"Peace I leave with you. My peace I give to you. I do not give to you as the world gives. Your heart must not be troubled or fearful."—John 14:27

The goal is a God-honoring peace. There will be always be strife in the midst of the battle, but in the end you are fighting for God's peace.

In what areas of your life are there war and you want peace?

_____

_____

_____

_____

_____

_____

_____

GO TO WAR

Pray for peace but pray as a fighter for peace. Don't give up. Be willing to sacrifice. Be determined. Seek resolution. Read 2 Corinthians 5:17–21. What does this say about what God has called you to do for Him?

WELCOME TO WAR

CHAPTER 7
READY FOR WAR

No, in all these things we are more than victorious through Him who loved us.—Romans 8:37

More than victorious.

How can we be MORE than victorious when we pray?

_____

_____

_____

_____

_____

Victory is good, but when God is involved, you can be more than victorious. You will learn more, grow more, and see more than you expected.

You will grow in patience.

You will gain more character, perseverance, and hope.

You will receive more experience.

You will be blessed and so will others.

You will see salvations.

You will witness deliverance from pain, suffering, and evil.

You will draw closer to God.

You will hear His plans for you.

You will sense fulfillment in life.

You will become less self-centered and more God-centered.

You will love people like never before.

So are you ready to go to war?

YES   **NO**

Before you start, WRITE OUT the top ten things you feel need prayer—areas you want to focus on—areas that trouble you the most. BE SPECIFIC.

Throughout this journal, keep those ten things in mind. We'll refer back to them again.

1. _____

2. _____

3. _____

4. _____

5. _____

6. _____

7. _____

8. _____

9. _____

10. _____

GO TO WAR

Pray for these ten areas right now. Know that the Commander in Chief hears you and He's going to work as you speak. Get ready to experience MORE than you imagined.

Now that you've committed to join God's prayer army and you're ready to go to war, it's time to get in shape. *Enter Boot Camp.*

BOOT CAMP

BOOT CAMP

CHAPTER 8
PRAYER TAKES DISCIPLINE

No discipline seems enjoyable at the time, but painful. Later on, however, it yields the fruit of peace and righteousness to those who have been trained by it.—Hebrews 12:11

When you enter Boot Camp, you agree to become a soldier in war, promising to defend your country.

Soldiers are no longer the people they used to be. They have new motivations and new purposes for living.

When you go to Boot Camp, you realize who you are and what you're made of.

You get down and dirty, in the mud, unafraid of cuts and scrapes.

In Boot Camp you find out who you really are and what you really believe.

In Boot Camp you realize your weaknesses and where you need to get stronger.

What are your strengths?

_____

_____

_____

_____

_____

_____

_____

What are your weaknesses?

_____

_____

_____

_____

_____

_____

_____

It's okay to have weaknesses. We cannot all be strong in all areas of our life. In Boot Camp you work on those weaknesses.

When it comes to prayer, we all have weaknesses, but it's not okay to just give up and say, "Well, I guess I'll never pray." Like anything else, praying faithfully requires discipline. You have to get in shape.

You commit yourself to get in shape so you can eventually become a warrior.

Think of all the things in your life that require discipline:

Sports   Music   Exercise   Writing   Reading the Bible

Other:_____

What is discipline?

Discipline takes TIME. By doing something over and over you begin to do it naturally.

Discipline takes TRAINING. You cannot instantly learn to do something overnight. Little by little you learn something new every day.

Discipline takes TENACITY. Some days you have to force yourself to do what you don't want to. By overcoming laziness, you grow tougher and tougher. Eventually the temptation to give up goes away.

Praying persistently and patiently requires discipline requires discipline. Time – Training – Tenacity.

You must give it time. How much? Start with a little and let it grow into more.

Every time you pray, God trains you to hear His voice more clearly. You'll know God's voice and direction plainly and easily.

Don't give up. Be strong and courageous. Push through the laziness.

So are you ready to get your prayer life into shape?

YES   **NO**

How much time can you commit to prayer to start?

_____

GO TO WAR

Ask God to help you be a better pray-er. Admit your weaknesses to Him. Tell Him you want to be a stronger soldier.

Write down what you believe God may be leading you to do to get stronger. . . .

_____

_____

_____

_____

_____

_____

BOOT CAMP

CHAPTER 9
PRAYING IS ABOUT A RELATIONSHIP

The LORD spoke with Moses face to face, just as a man speaks with his friend.—Exodus 33:11

Moses did something amazing. He hung out on a mountain with God. His relationship with God was so tight, the Bible compares it to a friendship.

Two times Moses spent forty-day periods with God. That's how close they were.

Praying is about relationship. You cannot have a relationship with someone and not spend time with them. You can't grow closer to someone unless you talk with them and share your feelings with them.

What do you talk to your friends about?

_____

_____

_____

_____

Do you talk about those same things with God? Why or why not?

_____

_____

_____

_____

_____

_____

God wants to hear about your day, your feelings, your ups and downs, your habits and hurts, the good and the bad. Because the more you communicate with Him, the more you show that you love Him and trust Him.

Look at this list of things you talk to your friends about. Do you talk to God about them?

School	Teachers	Classmates	Sports	Coaches
Games	Rivalries	Parents	Brothers	Sisters
Relatives	Neighbors	Car	Chores	Curfews
TV	Music	Concerts	Instagram	Facebook
Dancing	Movies	Videos	Alcohol	Drugs
Sex	Driving	College	Career	Marriage

Some of those things on the list seem dumb. You wonder, *Why would I talk to God about movies?*

Maybe you could pray about which movie God wants you to go see or avoid seeing.

Or pray that Hollywood makes better movies that honor Him?

Or pray about lessons that God could teach you after you saw a movie?

Now does praying about movies seem so dumb?

Do you think God is interested in EVERYTHING you have to say?

YES   **NO**   **MAYBE**

If God was not interested in your life, then you could make a case that He doesn't love you. But He does. Everything you do matters to Him and He wants you to come to Him to ask His advice.

Talking with a friend is natural and comfortable. You don't address your friend by saying, "O most gracious friend, who abidst with me and loveth me in thick and thin." You use everyday words in an everyday tone.

Just as you hang out with a friend, why can't you hang out with God?

GO TO WAR

Pray to God in a way that you would talk to a friend. Always be very respectful, but be open, natural, and conversational.

BOOT CAMP

CHAPTER 10
GOD IS . . .

In Boot Camp, you learn the basics. When you understand who God is—who you are praying to—then you understand how to pray.

To know God is to trust Him.

God is . . .

A Trinity—one God who reveals Himself in three persons (Matthew 28:19).

- God—the Father
- Jesus—the Son who died for you
- Holy Spirit—the teacher who lives in believers

Creator—He made the heavens and the earth.

Holy—He is without any sin.

Just—He is truthful and honest with all people.

Love—He loves all of mankind.

Our Judge—He judges people for their sins.

Power—He can do whatever He wants, when He wants.

Eternal—He has always existed and there has never been a time when He didn't.

Our Provider—He takes care of His children.

Our Healer—He heals hurts.

Which of those characteristics about God (and there are a bunch more) have you needed the most in your life?

_____

_____

_____

_____

_____

_____

_____

_____

_____

_____

_____

_____

_____

Each of those characteristics about God gives you a reason to pray to Him.

Trinity—He understands RELATIONSHIPS because He is a relationship.

Creator—He knows how to MAKE THINGS out of nothing.

Holy—He wants you to live a GODLY life.

Just—He wants you to be HONEST and RIGHTEOUS.

Love—He knows how hard it is to LOVE some people.

Our Judge—He knows about your SIN.

Power—He can give you STRENGTH.

Eternal—He wants you to live with Him FOREVER.

Our Provider—He knows we need FOOD, CLOTHES, AND SHELTER.

Our Healer—He knows our PAIN and sees our TEARS.

GO TO WAR

Pray to God according to a specific characteristic of God.
Believe that He knows how to help because it's who He is.

BOOT CAMP

CHAPTER 11

JESUS IS . . .

What separates all religions from each other is how they view Jesus Christ.

Check out His résumé found in Colossians 1:15–20. This is the real Jesus.

He is the image of the invisible God,

the firstborn over all creation.

For everything was created by Him,

in heaven and on earth,

the visible and the invisible,

whether thrones or dominions

or rulers or authorities—

all things have been created through Him and for Him.

He is before all things,

and by Him all things hold together.

He is also the head of the body, the church;

He is the beginning,

the firstborn from the dead,

so that He might come to have first place in everything.

For God was pleased to have

all His fullness dwell in Him,

and through Him to reconcile
everything to Himself
by making peace
through the blood of His cross—
whether things on earth or things in heaven.

So who is Jesus? According to this passage . . .

1. Jesus is God. The perfect image of God that we can touch and see.

2. Jesus enjoys the privileges of a firstborn—inheriting all things in a position of authority.[1]

3. Jesus created all things and all things were created for Him.

4. Jesus is eternal. He has always existed.

5. Jesus holds all things together. He's the glue that keeps the world intact.

6. Jesus was the first to die and resurrect, paving the way for others.

7. Jesus pleased the Father by what He did. Jesus fully represented God in flesh.

8. Jesus reconciled all believers with God. Sin separated everyone from God. Jesus provided a way to fix that.

9. Jesus brings peace, between people and God.

10. Jesus died for us. He went to battle and paid the price.

This is who you are praying to: Jesus who loves you and died for you. This is also who you are praying through to God the Father. Jesus is our way to God and mediator between us and God.

---

[1] Jesus was not created as this title seems to suggest, but Jesus was like a firstborn son who in ancient times received ownership and responsibility, sharing in His Father's authority.

He is the first and the last.

He was, is, and always will be.

He never changes.

He never lies.

He is always with us.

How does knowing the REAL Jesus change your prayer life?

_____

_____

_____

_____

_____

_____

_____

GO TO WAR

Pray through each characteristic of Jesus and thank Him for who He is.

BOOT CAMP

CHAPTER 12
YOU ARE A SINNER

For all have sinned and fall short of the glory of God.
—Romans 3:23

You are saved FROM something and saved INTO something. If you were drowning in the sea, you would want someone to pull you FROM the sea and INTO a boat or ONTO dry land. You have to cling to something that is sturdier than the sea.

We are all drowning in SIN. Starting with our very first sin, we get pulled under.

God is holy, and when we sin, we become unholy. He doesn't care if you're partially sinful, somewhat sinful, or heavily sinful. Any degree of sin and you're drowning, destined to die.

For the wages of sin is death, but the gift of God is eternal life in Christ Jesus our Lord.—Romans 6:23

Sin = death. Death is separation—from this earth, from our loved ones, from God.

But . . .

Christ = Life. The only way to find real life is through Him. If we come to Him, then we are reconciled to God and are no longer separated from Him.

For we know that our old self was crucified with Him in order that sin's dominion over the body may be abolished, so that we may no longer be enslaved to sin.—Romans 6:6

The Old Testament sacrifices were used to "cover" or "pay" for sins. Every sin has a death penalty.

One sin = One death penalty. 10,000 sins = One death penalty.

When we die, we have a debt to pay for our sin. God requires our death as payment. We spend an eternity paying for that sin in a place of eternal punishment and holy wrath. . . .

Hell.

However, Jesus offered to die for us. He took on the penalty of our "old self" and paid our debt through His crucifixion. He is an eternal God so His death has eternal consequences for everyone, for all time. Then He rose from the grave and reigns as King of kings and Lord of Lords!

Millions of your sins < God's grace.

Therefore, no condemnation now exists for those in Christ Jesus.—Romans 8:1

Now there is no condemnation—no death penalty—if you accept Jesus' death for your sins. His death MORE THAN pays for your sin. When you turn from your sins and trust in Jesus as your Lord, then . . .

- Sin does not separate you from God any longer.

- Sin cannot separate you from His love.

- Sin no longer separates you from life.

Your old sinful self . . . dead and gone.

A newly forgiven, restored self is born.

What you have to do now is BELIEVE that Jesus paid for all your sins, then ask Him for forgiveness and to give you a new heart. Then trust Him with your life. It is then that God saves you, forgives you, and makes you His child.

GO TO WAR

Pray confessing your sins and admitting that you are a sinner. Thank God for sending Jesus Christ to save you from your sins. Ask Jesus to save you, forgive you, change you, and to take control of your life.

BOOT CAMP

CHAPTER 13
YOU ARE SAVED

If you confess with your mouth, "Jesus is Lord," and believe in your heart that God raised Him from the dead, you will be saved.—Romans 10:9

To be saved you must CALL OUT.

ONE>>>>>>>You must declare that Jesus is Lord. BUT BEFORE YOU DO . . . remember this.

If Jesus is Lord . . .

- He's the boss. King of kings. Lord of lords. The General of generals.

- He knows best.

- He knows everything.

- His plan is ideal.

- He says you're a sinner so you must be.

Do you agree with that?

YES   **NO**

TWO>>>>>>>>You must believe that God raised Him from death. BUT BEFORE YOU DO . . . remember this.

If Jesus rose from the dead . . .

- Then God has power over death.

- Then you will be resurrected one day.

- Then He wants to have a relationship with you forever.

- Then your sins must be forgiven so you can be with God.

Are you okay with that?
YES   NO

So **IF** you CONFESS and you BELIEVE ,**THEN** the Bible says you are saved.

WHY?

If you have confessed that you need saving and believe and put your trust in Jesus to save you, then you will be saved.

"For the Son of Man has come to seek and to save the lost."
—Luke 19:10

Nobody comes to God unless God first draws them to Him. It was not your idea to love God. It was God's. On our own, we naturally, sinfully, only seek ourselves.

[Jesus said] "No one can come to Me unless the Father who sent Me draws him, and I will raise him up on the last day. It is written in the Prophets: And they will all be taught by God.

Everyone who has listened to and learned from the Father comes to Me—not that anyone has seen the Father except the One who is from God. He has seen the Father. I assure you: Anyone who believes has eternal life."—John 6:44–47

When someone enters BOOT CAMP, they enter a civilian and leave a soldier.

If you entered this journal a sinner, it's time you become a child of God, a believer, a follower, a warrior.

Soldiers take an oath. Christians do too.

GO TO WAR

- Tell God that you are a sinner.

- Tell God that you're sorry for your sins.

- Say that you believe Jesus is God and that He died for your sins.

- Say that you believe God will resurrect you one day.

- Tell God that you love Him and will serve Him.

- If you have done this, then receive God's forgiveness and know that you have become a child of God.

BOOT CAMP

CHAPTER 14
A GODLY LIFE

But have nothing to do with irreverent and silly myths. Rather, train yourself in godliness, for the training of the body has a limited benefit, but godliness is beneficial in every way, since it holds promise for the present life and also for the life to come.—1 Timothy 4:7–8

CONGRATULATIONS

If you believe everything you just prayed this week, THEN YOU HAVE GRADUATED BOOT CAMP.

You are ready to move on to the next stage of your prayer life.

Remember, you are a soldier. Soldiers train. While a soldier in the military trains his body and mind to be under the strict discipline of his duty during time of combat, a prayer warrior must train also.

That workout is known as godliness.

Face-to-face with temptation—choose godliness.

Battling depression and despair—choose godliness.

At war with selfishness—choose godliness.

Godliness is the most beneficial choice. The more you choose it, the stronger you become.

You, therefore, my son, be strong in the grace that is in Christ Jesus. And what you have heard from me in the presence of many witnesses, commit to faithful men who will be able to teach others also. Share in suffering as a good soldier of Christ Jesus. No one serving as a soldier gets entangled in the concerns of civilian life; he seeks to please the recruiter.
—2 Timothy 2:1–4

Paul told Timothy to . . .

1. Be strong, knowing that God's grace through Jesus Christ sustains us all.

2. Remember past teaching and God's Word.

3. Be surrounded by godly individuals who can teach you to do what is right.

4. Suffer as a soldier in the good fight for God.

5. Don't get wrapped up in earthly pleasures and desires.

6. Please the recruiter, God, who called you into battle.

You weren't saved just to be saved. You were saved to be a soldier and live an awesome, victorious, pure, and godly life.

GO TO WAR

Remember those ten prayers you offered in the last section? Rewrite them keeping in mind what you've learned so far.

1. _____

2. _____

3. _____

4. _____

5. _____

6. _____

7. _____

8. _____

9. _____

10. _____

It's time to look at the weapons in your prayer arsenal. You are armed and dangerous!

THE
ARSENAL

Every soldier needs weapons in his arsenal and he has to learn how to operate those weapons.

List all the weapons you can think of that a soldier could carry when going into war.

_____

_____

_____

_____

_____

_____

_____

_____

A prayer warrior has weapons too. He needs to know all the weapons in his arsenal to be the most effective.

Before we begin, what weapons do you THINK a prayer warrior has?

_____

_____

_____

_____

_____

_____

_____

Let's take a look at a prayer warrior's arsenal and how to use them.

THE ARSENAL

CHAPTER 15
WEAPON #1: GOD'S WORD

Read these verses about God's Word.

God—His way is perfect; the word of the Lord is pure.
He is a shield to all who take refuge in Him.—Psalm 18:30

Praise the Lord, all His angels of great strength, who do His
word, obedient to His command.—Psalm 103:20

He sent His word and healed them; He rescued them from
the Pit.—Psalm 107:20

Your word is a lamp for my feet, a light on my path.
—Psalm 119:105

For the word of God is living and effective and sharper than
any double-edged sword, penetrating as far as the separation
of soul and spirit, joints and marrow. It is able to judge the
ideas and thoughts of the heart.—Hebrews 4:12

How do the verses on the previous page describe God's Word like a weapon?

_____

_____

_____

_____

_____

_____

_____

_____

God's Word SHIELDS a believer with truth.

God's Word is like a SWORD, cutting through the lies.

God's Word calls on reinforcements, ANGELS.

God's Word RESCUES people from the grave.

God's Word is LIGHT needed to see into the darkness.

When you pray, PRAY GOD'S WORD. When Jesus was under attack by Satan in the desert, He didn't resort to karate chops and kung fu. Jesus spoke Scriptures back at Satan. Scripture is Jesus' weapon. Why would you use anything else?

God's Word is TRUTH, and as we know about the Enemy, Satan hates truth. He feeds off lies. Lies are Satan's weapons. Truth exposes his intentions and defeats his advances.

You cannot focus on what YOU think or feel is true and right, but on what GOD says is truth and righteousness.

Psalms is an excellent place to start. The prayers in that book are cries out to God for help and deliverance.

GO TO WAR

PICK A PSALM, any psalm. Read it as a prayer.

Which psalm did you pick?_____

When you prayed the psalm, how did it feel different from your own prayer?

_____

_____

_____

_____

_____

THE ARSENAL

CHAPTER 16
WEAPON #2: PRAISE

Hallelujah!
Praise God in His sanctuary.
Praise Him in His mighty heavens.
Praise Him for His powerful acts;
praise Him for His abundant greatness.
Praise Him with trumpet blast;
praise Him with harp and lyre.
Praise Him with tambourine and dance;
praise Him with flute and strings.
Praise Him with resounding cymbals;
praise Him with clashing cymbals.
Let everything that breathes praise the Lord.
Hallelujah!—Psalm 150

Praise is acknowledging, honoring, and worshiping the qualities of God.

Why should we praise God? Does God want praise? Does He need to know He's doing a good job?

_____

_____

_____

_____

_____

_____

_____

_____

_____

We all like to be praised. We like to know we're doing a good job. Much of our need for praise comes from our insecurity. We want to feel better as people point out our good qualities. God is not insecure.

He knows who He is and what is right. He does not need to impress anyone because He is already the greatest, the most powerful, eternal, exceedingly perfect being that has ever lived. God does not need praise. He deserves praise!

If we praise God, who are we not praising?

_____

_____

_____

_____

_____

_____

_____

_____

Praise directs our focus to His qualities. If we don't praise God, we will praise something else. Something far less deserving. We were made to elevate something in our lives and give it our full attention—God. However, usually in this sinful world, that attention turns to ourselves. We call it selfishness or self-praise.

Think of your favorite singer or a band that you love. You go to their concert. They come out on stage and play your favorite song. You scream and clap and sing along. You may love the band so much, you cry out for them to do an encore.

Does God get that kind of praise in your life now?

YES   **NO**

Why or why not?

_____

_____

_____

_____

_____

Is there anything in your life that you delight in and adore more than God?

_____

_____

_____

_____

_____

Praise directs us to where our hearts need to be centered. Praise draws our time and attention.

If we praise God, we don't praise ourselves and we don't praise other things that will only let us down and weaken us. We benefit from praising God!

When Jesus entered Jerusalem the week before His crucifixion, the people lined the streets praising Him. The Pharisees demanded that Jesus stop them from such praise.

He answered, "I tell you, if they were to keep silent, the stones would cry out!"—Luke 19:40

The world needs to praise God—even the rocks—but the Enemy will always try to stop it. Resist the temptation to praise anything else.

GO TO WAR

PRAISE GOD right now, listing every reason you can think of.

_____

_____

_____

_____

_____

_____

_____

THE ARSENAL

CHAPTER 17

WEAPON #3: CONFESSION

How joyful is the one
whose transgression is forgiven,
whose sin is covered!
How joyful is the man
the LORD does not charge with sin
and in whose spirit is no deceit!
When I kept silent, my bones became brittle
from my groaning all day long.
For day and night Your hand was heavy on me;
my strength was drained
as in the summer's heat. Selah
Then I acknowledged my sin to You
and did not conceal my iniquity.
I said, "I will confess my transgressions to the LORD,"
and You took away the guilt of my sin.—Psalm 32:1–5

A soldier treks long miles. He must be equipped but he must not carry extra weight. Extra weight slows a body down, tires a soldier out, decreases his effectiveness.

A Christian warrior needs to get rid of the things weighing him or her down.

Guilt is that burden.

The Enemy wants you to feel guilty. Carrying guilt is like throwing bricks into your backpack. Guilt makes a prayer warrior ineffective.

If you got rid of guilt, what could you do better than ever before?

_____

_____

_____

_____

_____

_____

_____

_____

You're guilty. You know it. We all are. God knows it. But you don't have to feel guilty.

And many who had become believers came confessing and disclosing their practices.—Acts 19:18

Believers confess. The minute they encounter a purely holy God they immediately recognize their own impurity and unholiness. They want to distance themselves from their sin.

So lighten your load and confess. Turn it over to Him.

Once you know you are forgiven, the burden falls off. You are free.

How does that happen?

As far as the east is from the west, so far has He removed our transgressions from us.—Psalm 103:12

Once you confess your sins—admitting your role in the sin and assigning the blame entirely on yourself—you've acknowledged the truth. Sins begin with lies. Truth destroys the lies. Confession applies truth to the sinful lies.

After we confess, we ask for forgiveness. To be forgiven, the debt of our sin must be paid. Jesus paid that debt by dying on the cross for our sins.

When we repent and trust in Jesus, God accepts Jesus' payment of death for our sins, and then He no longer sees us as sinners. The sinful stigma is removed from us—as far as the east is from west. How far is that? East and west are total opposites. They never meet.

That's how far your sins are removed from you.

GO TO WAR

ASK GOD TO FORGIVE YOU OF ALL YOUR SINS. ASK GOD TO HELP YOU NEVER DO THEM AGAIN.

You confessed. God forgave.

It's over and done with, no longer on God's record books.

He's not going to look at it. Why should you?

Enjoy the freedom and peace of His forgiveness! You never have to go back to that sin again.

THE ARSENAL

CHAPTER 18
WEAPON #4: PASSION

When people from the Bible prayed, they really poured it all out.

On the twenty-fourth day of this month the Israelites assembled; they were fasting, wearing sackcloth, and had put dust on their heads.—Nehemiah 9:1

Why do you think people went to such extremes to pray?

_____

_____

_____

_____

_____

_____

If outsiders saw this kind of passion, they would probably not attend church or want to be a Christian. Who wants to not eat, wear itchy clothes, and get all dirty?

Or, do you think this kind of passion would attract people to God?

_____

_____

_____

_____

People might even be drawn to God when they see this kind of passion in a person's life.

If you passionately love God, God becomes a priority. The Enemy can't squeeze in or interrupt that love.

"He [Jesus] answered, 'Love the Lord your God with all your heart, with all your soul, with all your strength, and with all your mind; and your neighbor as yourself.'"—Luke 10:27

What are differences between HEART, SOUL, STRENGTH, and MIND?

HEART: your core beliefs, passions, desires, interests, focus, and commitments

SOUL: your attitudes and emotions

STRENGTH: your determination and forcefulness

MIND: your thoughts, choices, and decisions

The Enemy wants you to maybe just "LIKE" God . . . "FAVOR" God . . . "ACT" godly.

The Enemy doesn't want you to PASSIONATELY LOVE THE LORD YOUR GOD WITH ALL YOUR HEART, SOUL, STRENGTH, and MIND. No way.

Your heart of passion becomes a force the Enemy can't penetrate.

Sadly, many terrorists are more committed to their false causes than Christians are to the One true God. These misguided fanatics are willing to sacrifice it all for what they think is right. Satan has convinced them to passionately commit their lives to a lie.

A Christian knows the truth. You cannot commit half-heartedly to something. It's not really commitment. It's a hobby or a pastime. A passion gets all of you, all the time.

Your heart can be like an explosive time bomb of passion. Blow up the Enemy's intention by giving your entire heart, soul, strength, and mind to God.

GO TO WAR

Pray specifically for all four parts of yourself—heart, soul, strength, and mind. Ask that God perfectly balances you in all four areas. These four areas may seem minor in their differences, but they make sure there is no gap to allow doubt or apathy to creep in.

THE ARSENAL

CHAPTER 19
WEAPON #5: THANKFULNESS

Fill in the word that fits in the blanks. (HINT: it's the same word or a derivative of the same word.)

I will _____ the LORD for His righteousness; I will sing about the name of Yahweh the Most High.—Psalm 7:17

Enter His gates with _____ and His courts with praise. Give _____ to Him and praise His name.—Psalm 100:4

I will give _____ to You because You have answered me and have become my salvation.—Psalm 118:21

Give _____ to the LORD, for He is good. His love is eternal. —Psalm 136:1

Are you a thankful person? Do you remember to say "thank you"?

_____

_____

_____

_____

_____

How do you say thanks to people?

_____

_____

_____

_____

_____

_____

_____

_____

Can you be thankful without saying "thanks"?

_____

_____

_____

_____

If you don't say thanks, what are you quietly saying?

_____

_____

_____

_____

Thankfulness is a weapon because it acknowledges who truly provides everything you need and everything you have.

Praise and thanks in the Bible are closely aligned, though other times they are seen as separate. For the sake of our prayer time, we will call them two different things.

- **Praise acknowledges the qualities of God and who He is (loving, gracious, forgiving, merciful, etc.)**

- **Thankfulness acknowledges what God has done and has provided you (relationships, finances, food, clothes, shelter, etc.)**

If you don't thank God, you'll end up becoming prideful, greedy, or lustful and tend to give yourself credit for the good things in your life.

As you thank yourself, you begin to praise yourself. You will tend to see yourself as the provider and the super-power that gets things done.

Thankfulness sees everything you have on earth as a gift from God.

There are many ways to show appreciation, but one primary way to say "thanks," and that's to SAY IT.

"Thank You, God, for giving me . . ."

So weave THANKFULNESS all throughout your prayer time. It's a weapon against self-appreciation that truthfully sees God as the source of everything. Gratefulness brings contentment and joy!

GO TO WAR

Go to the Thank You page (page 218) at the back of this journal and list all the reasons to thank God. Refer to this page often to remind yourself of reasons to thank Him. Add to this page in the weeks to come.

THE ARSENAL

CHAPTER 20
WEAPON #6: PRAY FOR OTHERS AND YOURSELF

First of all, then, I urge that petitions, prayers, intercessions, and thanksgivings be made for everyone.—1 Timothy 2:1

Praying for Others!

Most people think this is the only thing prayer is about. The list of "TO-DO's" God needs to do.

Those in the hospital. Hurting. Dying.

Those in the unemployment line. Financial ruin. Unpaid bills.

The lost. Unsaved. Deceived. Confused.

The brokenhearted. Sad. Alone. Depressed.

Only one part of prayer is really about prayer requests, the things that we want God to do for us or for others.

IN FACT, WE SHOULD LOAD UP ON THE OTHER WEAPONS FIRST THEN WRAP UP WITH OUR PRAYER REQUESTS:

_____

_____

_____

_____

_____

_____

_____

_____

Prayer requests are only one part of the artillery. It's not the only thing.

PRAYING FOR OTHERS does not:

- Alert God about something He doesn't know about.

- Give God some ideas He hadn't thought about.

- Boss God around and tell Him what He needs to do.

PRAYING FOR OTHERS works because:

- It focuses your heart on the needs of others.

- It comforts others to know they are being prayed for.

- It shows God that you cannot find a solution, but only He can.

- It may lead to a solution as God speaks to you about what to do.

Praying for Yourself!

It seems arrogant and selfish to pray for yourself, but you need to.

Do you have needs and requests? Sure.

Does God care about those as much as He cares about others? Absolutely!

MAKE SURE YOU AREN'T ONLY PRAYING ABOUT YOURSELF ALL THE TIME. A self-centered warrior is ineffective in God's army!

In fact, if you go through all the other weapons in your prayer artillery, by the time you get to you, you've gotten PERSPECTIVE on your situation and SURRENDERED yourself fully to Him. That's what God wants.

Many people spend all their time praying about themselves. Don't make prayer time ALL ABOUT YOU. Make it first and foremost about God.

Did Paul pray for himself? Sure, but most times he asked others to pray for him as he prayed for others.

PRAYER TIME SHOULD BE OUTWARDLY FOCUSED but it has inward benefits for us too.

GO TO WAR

Turn to page 211 of the War Room Journal at the back of the book. Begin to list the needs of others that you hear about and that you prayed for. Refer back to those needs. When you hear an answer to that prayer (you may need to contact people to find out the resolution), mark it and date it. List your needs too and the answers that come.

THE ARSENAL

CHAPTER 21
WEAPON #7: PERSISTENCE

Pray constantly. Give thanks in everything, for this is God's will for you in Christ Jesus. Don't stifle the Spirit.
—1 Thessalonians 5:17–19

Jesus told this parable about a widow. Widows, in ancient times, were considered weak. They received very little respect and had no authority.

However, this one widow knew how to get things done.

Jesus told them a parable on the need for them to pray always and not become discouraged:

There was a judge in a certain town who didn't fear God or respect man. And a widow in that town kept coming to him, saying, "Give me justice against my adversary."

For a while he was unwilling, but later he said to himself, "Even though I don't fear God or respect man, yet because this widow keeps pestering me, I will give her justice, so she doesn't wear me out by her persistent coming."

Then the Lord said, "Listen to what the unjust judge says. Will not God grant justice to His elect who cry out to Him day and night?

Will He delay to help them? I tell you that He will swiftly grant them justice. Nevertheless, when the Son of Man comes, will He find that faith on earth?"—Luke 18:1–8

How would you describe the widow? Pushy? Bossy? Annoying? Something else . . . ?

_____

_____

_____

_____

_____

_____

_____

To the judge she was annoying.

But her persistence showed her passion for justice.

If you pray persistently, God doesn't roll His eyes and say, "Not this again!"

But He wants you to be passionate, not annoying.

What's the difference between a passionate prayer and an annoying prayer?

_____

_____

_____

_____

_____

_____

_____

Passionate prayer—you want the things God wants.

Annoying prayer—you want the things you want.

A little ol' widow got a mean ol' judge to get something done for her through her persistence.

If a mean ol' judge can be moved by persistence, couldn't a kindly Father in heaven be moved too?

Use the weapon of persistence and don't give up when you see troubles ahead.

Keep praying and never stop.

GO TO WAR

You are twenty-one days into prayer training. If you made it this far, it's safe to say you are a persistent person. However, you're not even half way through the experience. Don't give up. Stay focused. Keep praying.

Remember those ten prayers? How are things going? Any answers? Rewrite them keeping in mind what you've learned so far.

1. _____

2. _____

3. _____

4. _____

5. _____

6. _____

7. _____

8. _____

9. _____

10. _____

Now you know what weapons you have at your disposal. It's time to learn how to use them. *Welcome to Basic Training.*

BASIC TRAINING

Your instructor for Basic Training today is a man named MATTHEW.

Matthew trained with the best prayer warrior of all—Jesus Christ. In fact, he loved so much what Jesus had to say about prayer, he featured the information in his manual, the Gospel of Matthew.

For the Basic Prayer Training, let's start with Matthew 6, then move back to Matthew 5.

First we'll focus on our ATTITUDE in prayer, then the ELEMENTS of prayer.

BASIC TRAINING

CHAPTER 22
PRAY SINCERELY

"Whenever you pray, you must not be like the hypocrites, because they love to pray standing in the synagogues and on the street corners to be seen by people. I assure you: They've got their reward."—Matthew 6:5

Hypocrites pretend to be one thing when they are really another.

A praying hypocrite pretends to glorify God when he's really glorifying himself. He wants people to see him pray so they can think, *Wow, what a spiritual person.* The hypocrite doesn't have to speak out loud. His actions speak volumes.

A hypocrite wants the world to see him ACT all righteous, yet he doesn't want to BE righteous because that's too hard.

Jesus said a hypocritical, it's-all-about-me-being-in-the-spotlight kind of pray-er has already gotten his full reward.

What do you think is the FULL REWARD?

_____

_____

_____

_____

_____

(HINT: The reward comes from earth, not heaven.)

Showmanship has no place in the Christian life. You cannot draw attention to yourself and expect God to be glorified.

If you pray publicly, ask yourself these questions:

- Am I praying to lead people corporately to the throne of God?

- Am I seeking to please God or people?

- Am I listening to the Holy Spirit, or am I saying things people want to hear?

So does that mean someone should never pray out loud? No, of course not. It's all about attitude and purpose and passion when you pray.

While Ezra prayed and confessed, weeping and falling face-down before the house of God, an extremely large assembly of Israelite men, women, and children gathered around him. The people also wept bitterly.—Ezra 10:1

Ezra made quite a spectacle of himself while praying. Was he trying to draw attention to himself? Was he a hypocrite? NO and NO.

Ezra was passionate, and people saw his passion and joined him in his passion. His public prayer turned the nation around. We can pray in public but with the right motivation.

You may be a shy person thinking, *I'll never draw attention to myself in crowds or on stage, so I'm good here.*

But insincerity can occur quietly when nobody's looking. The attitude of a person's prayer life could lack sincerity. In your own mind, you could put yourself center stage, drawing all the attention to yourself. You could be mouthing words but completely ignoring God in your heart.

What is the prayer test for sincerity?

- Am I praying for God's will and not my will?

- Am I praying out of love for the person/people I'm praying for?

- Do I want what's best for them?

- Does my reward mean less than what will benefit God and others?

If you can pray this way, pure of heart and motives, then you can pray sincerely.

Write out an insincere prayer.

_____

_____

_____

_____

_____

_____

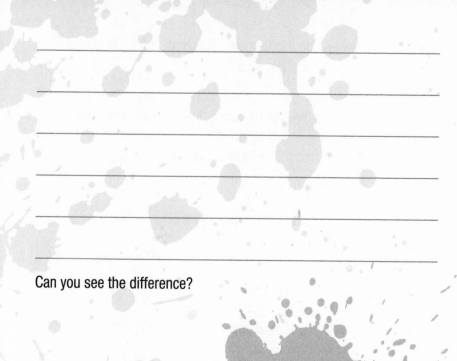

_____

_____

_____

_____

_____

_____

Can you see the difference?

GO TO WAR

Now pray sincerely, keeping in mind the checklist of sincerity, making sure your motives and desires are removed from your prayer time.

BASIC TRAINING

CHAPTER 23
PRAY SECRETLY

"But when you pray, go into your private room, shut your door, and pray to your Father who is in secret. And your Father who sees in secret will reward you."—Matthew 6:6

What are the advantages of praying in a closet or a private room?

_____

_____

_____

_____

_____

_____

Why are private "closet prayers" rewarded by God?

_____

_____

_____

_____

_____

Your closet is a small, forgotten side room that stores stuff. It's not a dining room with fine china or a family room with an expensive TV. There's very little glamor in a closet. We tend to hide things there from the public, especially when company drops in.

But imagine how cluttered your house would be without a closet. Stuff thrown everywhere. Piles of junk under your feet. You put things in a closet to make your life more organized and free.

Closet prayers are like closets.

Closet prayers are about _intimacy_. Small. One-on-one. Just you and God. You want nothing else and no one else in that tight space.

Closet prayers are about _humility_. It's not about the glamor of the big rooms. It's about utility and function.

Closet prayers are about _secrets_. We share our secrets with God in prayer, exposing them to Him so He can forgive and heal us.

Closet prayers are about _storage_. We get rid of the clutter in our life and lay everything out before God in prayer. We store those concerns with Him and remove them out from under our feet.

So when you pray . . .

- **Get close to God.**

- **Humble yourself before Him.**

- **Share with Him your secrets.**

- **Store all your needs with Him and leave them there.**

Finding a "Prayer Closet" tells God that you dedicate one part of your house solely to Him. We have rooms for all kinds of things—trophies, favorite teams, hobbies. Why not a place for God?

GO TO WAR

Find a closet or private room right now, close the door, and pray. Then write about the experience.

_____

_____

_____

Do you want to do this more often?

BASIC TRAINING

CHAPTER 24
PRAY SUCCINCTLY

"When you pray, don't babble like the idolaters, since they imagine they'll be heard for their many words."—Matthew 6:7

You probably know some babblers in your life. People that come up to you and go on and on and on and on . . .

What do you think about babblers?

_____

_____

_____

_____

_____

_____

_____

You probably think . . .

- They care only about themselves and not others.
- They are so ME focused and not WE focused.
- They could be talking to a wall and it wouldn't make a difference.
- They think the more words they throw at something the greater the solution.

You probably don't want to be around these kinds of people.

Babblers sometimes apply their many-word-strategy to their prayers. Why do they do that?

- They may want people to be impressed by their vocabulary.
- They may want to draw attention to their spiritual expertise.
- They want to interject themselves into everything they say.

Do MORE WORDS mean MORE BLESSING by God?

YES   **NO**

Do MORE WORDS mean MORE ATTENTION by God?

YES   **NO**

It's not just about the time you spend praying. It's about effectiveness.

Getting specific and to the point.

Being more passionate, sincere, and focused.

Why can you listen to one speaker for an hour and love every minute of it and listen to another speaker for an hour and lose track of what they are saying?

- Content
- Commitment
- Quick and to the point
- Word choice

Is it possible for two people to pray one hour each and one's prayer time be more efficient, better connected, more sincere, more passionate than the other's? Yes.

Write out a babbling prayer.

_____

_____

_____

_____

_____

_____

_____

_____

_____

_____

_____

_____

Write out that same prayer succinctly.

_____

_____

_____

Do you see the difference?

GO TO WAR

Choose your words carefully when you pray. Do not substitute more words for more passion. Get to the point powerfully and precisely. Don't just try to get done more quickly. Pray more effectively.

BASIC TRAINING

CHAPTER 25
PRAY ANTICIPATING

"Don't be like them, for your Father knows the things you need before you ask Him."—Matthew 6:8

If we pray believing God already knows, that should change the way we pray. How?

_____

_____

_____

_____

_____

_____

_____

What should we anticipate when we pray to God?

_____

_____

_____

_____

_____

_____

_____

Many times we pray and wonder, What's the use? Just more time spent talking to air. Nothing ever gets done. No solutions ever found. The same ol' same ol'.

This happens when we are not walking by faith and lose our anticipation.

Look at this story of Anna, a prophetess in the temple during the time of Christ's birth.

There was also a prophetess, Anna, a daughter of Phanuel, of the tribe of Asher. She was well along in years, having lived with her husband seven years after her marriage, and was a widow for 84 years. She did not leave the temple complex, serving God night and day with fasting and prayers.

At that very moment, she came up and began to thank God and to speak about Him to all who were looking forward to the redemption of Jerusalem.—Luke 2:36–38

It's hard to say how long Anna had been praying for hope to come to Jerusalem, but from this passage we can assume it was a long time. Eighty years? That's 29,200 days. Every day she went to the temple expecting God to do something.

Then one day it happened. The Christ child showed up. Imagine if she gave up the day before and missed Him. The one day Mary and Joseph brought their firstborn to the temple for dedication and she could have given up the day before.

Every day Anna anticipated. One day she received the focus of her anticipation.

Anticipation makes praying fun. Every morning you can't wait to see what God is going to do next. You wake up ready to discover God at work. Without anticipation, we grow weary and resent prayer, thinking it's useless.

If you pray with anticipation, you know . . .

- **God hears you.**

- **God is going to work.**

- **God has something to tell you.**

- **God has the solution.**

- **The solution is coming.**

If you pray this way every day, praying takes on a whole new meaning.

GO TO WAR

Pray anticipating, knowing that God is at work and the solution is coming. Don't allow the Enemy to tell you God does not hear and nothing ever comes of praying. Pray believing that God is working and that in His perfect timing, the solution will surely come.

THE MODEL PRAYER

Now let's move on to the specifics. The words. In what way should we pray? Jesus offered this model . . .

"Therefore you should pray like this:

Our Father in heaven,

Your name be honored as holy.

Your kingdom come.

Your will be done,

on earth as it is in heaven.

Give us today our daily bread.

And forgive us our debts,

as we also have forgiven our debtors.

And do not bring us into temptation,

but deliver us from the evil one."

—Matthew 6:9–13

Remember, prayers are not supposed to be babbling and repetitious memorizations without thinking about the words. The words are important. So is the heart.

Jesus gave a MODEL to pray, saying, "Include these important thoughts and ideas into your prayer," not "Just say these words and it will act as some sort of magical Abracadabra."

So let's look at each important part of this prayer and model our own prayer like this.

BASIC TRAINING

CHAPTER 26
"OUR FATHER"

"Not everyone who says to Me, 'Lord, Lord!' will enter the kingdom of heaven, but only the one who does the will of My Father in heaven."—Matthew 7:21

The Model Prayer begins by establishing your relationship with the One you are praying to.

Your Creator. Your spiritual Father.

An earthly father is expected to:

- Love and care for the family

- Provide for their needs

- Offer security and protection

- Be a guide, mentor, and teacher

- Bless, lead, and pass on a legacy

Your spiritual Father performs the same role:

- He loves and cares for you

- He provides for your needs

- He offers security against harm

- He is a guide and teacher

- He wants you to carry on a spiritual legacy to future generations

Why does the prayer begin with "Our" Father, not "My" Father?

_____

_____

_____

_____

_____

While God is your Father, He's also the Father of all Christians (John 1:12). This helps us to understand that we are all connected through one very important relationship. This brings unity to our prayer. We are not alone. God is speaking to all His children at the same time.

What other titles could God demand we use that would change the prayer?

_____

_____

_____

_____

_____

What if you started your prayer with Our Boss? Too cold. It's all about the work.

What if you started your prayer with Our Buddy? Very informal. Makes you almost an equal and you could lose respect.

The title Father deserves respect while keeping the sense of intimacy. So pray to your Father, the one who created you and gave you life, shaping you into the person you are today.

He can't wait to hear from you.

GO TO WAR

Hopefully your time with your earthly father is good and healthy, with some memories that you can ponder. Think about those times (and thank God for them) but apply them to your relationship with your heavenly Father. Time spent having fun, talking, learning, watching. See your heavenly Father as much more loving, perfect, and powerful than your earthly father.

You may need to forgive your earthly father at some point. Pray for those who don't have a father that they find a heavenly Father.

BASIC TRAINING

CHAPTER 27
"IN HEAVEN"

The Lord looks down from heaven; He observes everyone.
—Psalm 33:13

God looks down from heaven on the human race to see if there is one who is wise, one who seeks God.—Psalm 53:2

Not only are we praying to our Father, but our Father in heaven.

Why is it important that we recognize that God is in heaven?

_____

_____

_____

_____

_____

_____

Heaven is about *perspective*. The higher the view, the greater the scope. God sees the big picture, not just our point of view, which is limited and skewed. We pray to a God who can understand all the pieces and parts and how they all fit together. From heaven, you cannot only see the present, but the future (the past too).

Heaven is about *holiness*. God has an incorruptible view of our situation. Sin and selfishness do not cloud the situation like it does on earth.

Heaven is about *eternity*. It is in heaven where we will be when we die. On earth we see a temporary view of things with short-lived promises. Heaven gives us the forever reasons and eternal ramifications of events.

When we pray, we want a heavenly view of life!

What does heaven mean to you?

_____

_____

_____

_____

_____

_____

_____

_____

Praying to your Father in heaven changes your perspective when you pray.

As God looks down on our lives, we need to look up and see our world as He sees it.

It's a much better view from up there.

GO TO WAR

As you pray, imagine seeing your prayers from God's point of view in heaven. How do they seem? Pray for the proper perspective, holiness, and eternity in our lives.

BASIC TRAINING

CHAPTER 28
"HIS HOLINESS"

As obedient children, do not be conformed to the desires of your former ignorance. But as the One who called you is holy, you also are to be holy in all your conduct; for it is written, Be holy, because I am holy.—1 Peter 1:14–16

The word *holy* means "set apart, sacred." It describes something not contaminated by the world or infected by sin.

God is holy because He is not of this world and not stained by sin. He is pure and right in all that He does.

As part of our prayer time, we must be reminded that "Your name be honored as holy." When we pray, we enter a sacred time with a sinless God. This is no casual conversation with a friend online. This is the one and only Lord.

We should speak to Him with holy mouths.

We should seek His holy purposes.

We should respect His holy decisions.

What does it mean when it says HIS NAME is holy?

It means His reputation is holy. He always has been and always will be pure and sinless. His works are holy. If God puts His stamp of approval on something, it's the perfect plan. Holiness is who He is. It defines God.

How would our prayer change if God were not holy or only partially holy?

_____

_____

_____

_____

_____

_____

We would not be able to trust an unholy God. We would fear His motivations. An unholy God would only have His own desires in mind . . . not ours.

Scary thought.

In the Bible, God calls His people to be holy. Holiness is not for God alone. We should seek holiness in our lives. This means . . .

- **Everything we do, in thought and deed, is pure and righteous.**

- **Every part of our lives shows that God is most important to us.**

- **Every moment is a sacred time, set aside for God.**

Our prayer time is a HOLY time with a HOLY God seeking His HOLY desires.

If God is holy, does it change what we pray about?

_____

_____

_____

_____

_____

_____

GO TO WAR

READ ISAIAH 6 and see yourself in the throne room of God, as the angels proclaim Him to be "holy, holy, holy." Pay attention to how everyone treats God and what God wants Isaiah to communicate to the people. Pray accordingly.

BASIC TRAINING

CHAPTER 29
"HIS KINGDOM COME AND WILL BE DONE"

"The time is fulfilled, and the kingdom of God has come near; repent and believe in the good news!" —Mark 1:15

We must want God's kingdom to come to this earth and remove the current kingdom that rules here presently.

The worldly kingdom, influenced by human will and Satan's desires, is only causing the slow deterioration of all moral values and the destruction of souls. This current kingdom infiltrates homes, schools, and governments, slowly removing God from our culture.

If God's kingdom were to come to earth, how would that change the world?

_____

_____

_____

_____

_____

When you pray, do you want your will or God's will to be done?

God's will   **My will**

Praying for God's will to be done means you are willing for your will not to be done. It means that you surrender fully and completely to whatever God wants you to do.

Jesus came as the perfect model of surrender to God's will. Read Jesus' words.

"I can do nothing on My own. I judge only as I hear, I judge, and My judgment is righteous, because I do not seek My own will but the will of Him who sent me."—John 5:30

"For I have come down from heaven, not to do My will, but the will of Him who sent Me."—John 6:38

Going a little farther, He fell facedown and prayed, "My Father! If it be possible, let this cup pass from Me. Yet not as I will, but as You will."—Matthew 26:39

Jesus didn't just come to earth and tell us to do God's will; He sought God's will also. But we wonder, How hard was that? Jesus is God, so wouldn't it be natural for Him to do God's will?

Yes, but remember He came to earth in human flesh and fought against the will of the weak, human condition. By living in the world, He put Himself in a position to be tempted just like us. He showed us that we could successfully overcome self-will and seek God's will while living on earth

There is a way for God's kingdom to come to this earth. Jesus showed us how.

GO TO WAR

READ MATTHEW 26:36–46. See how Jesus prayed with passion. Notice the contrast with the disciples. Whose will were they seeking? Pray for God's will and don't doze off instead.

BASIC TRAINING

CHAPTER 30

"ON EARTH AS IT IS IN HEAVEN"

"Then Jesus came near and said to them, 'All authority has been given to Me in heaven and on earth.'"—Matthew 28:18

At creation, heaven and earth were united in obeying God's will. God ruled on earth in the same way He ruled heaven.

Then something went very wrong.

Sin entered that paradise and brought death upon the earth. Selfishness and sin began to reign in hearts rather than love and righteousness. Sin seeped into the very DNA of humans, passing from one generation to another.

Now, what happened on earth looked nothing like what happened in heaven.

But God had a plan.

He sent Jesus to earth to begin the process of realigning earth with heaven. In its sinful state, earth was doomed. Now the forgiveness of sins through Jesus' death on the cross did more than pay for our sins; it made a way to restore the earth as well.

It will take effort . . . from all of us.

Slowly, one prayer and one decision at a time, heaven can regain new ground on earth.

If earth was "as it is in" heaven, how would it be different?

_____

_____

_____

_____

_____

_____

Ultimately the only way earth can become "as it is in" heaven will be when Jesus Christ returns and officially ends sin's reign. It will take a total reboot and a complete, ultimate, extreme makeover.

But the Day of the Lord will come like a thief; on that day the heavens will pass away with a loud noise, the elements will burn and be dissolved, and the earth and the works on it will be disclosed. Since all these things are to be destroyed in this way, it is clear what sort of people you should be in holy conduct and godliness as you wait for and earnestly desire the coming of the day of God. The heavens will be on fire

and be dissolved because of it, and the elements will melt with the heat. But based on His promise, we wait for the new heavens and a new earth, where righteousness will dwell.
—2 Peter 3:10–13

On that day, God's kingdom will be eternally established on heaven and earth, but in the meantime we should pray for more earth to become more like heaven on earth, in our hearts, in our homes, in our churches, and in our cities. God can take more ground with every new believer and every godly choice.

This is the war we fight. Taking the earth for heaven. This is the battle line your prayers defend.

GO TO WAR

Pray for God's kingdom to come to earth. Pray that His rule would change your life now. Your family. Your school. Your church. Your government. Pray for Christ's return one day and all that needs to occur before that happens.

BASIC TRAINING

CHAPTER 31
"OUR DAILY BREAD"

"This is why I tell you: Don't worry about your life, what you will eat or what you will drink; or about your body, what you will wear. Isn't life more than food and the body more than clothing?"—Matthew 6:25

For our time of prayer, the phrase "Our daily bread" stands not only for food, but for all provisions that we need and receive from God.

We can ask for the necessities of life when we pray—food, drink, and clothing. According to just a few verses after Jesus' model prayer, He makes this statement in Matthew 6:25 about our provisions.

"Don't worry. I've got you covered," Jesus seems to say.

So our prayer should not be a worrisome prayer, pleading with God to take care of our needs. He's promised to help. Trust Him. It's a simple task.

But we can't take it for granted, expecting food and clothing to just be there. We should pray and rely on God, and when it's there for us, we need to see it as an answer to our prayer.

Are you thankful for every meal you eat?
YES   **NO**

Part of our prayer life needs to include our prayer before we eat. It is important to stop and say thanks.

And why is giving thanks limited to just meals?

Why not give thanks before you take a drink of water at the fountain? "Thank You, God, for this drink of water."

Or when you buy clothes at the store? "Thank You, God, for these jeans."

Or when you take a bite of a snack? "Thank You, God, for this treat."

Even in our nondinner prayers, it's a good time to thank God for our provisions too. Millions of people go to bed hungry. Millions are homeless. Millions are malnourished. Millions die without water. It makes you rethink all those daily EXPECTATIONS you have.

You're being blessed by every drink of water you take, every bite of food you eat, every time you put on clothes.

The prayer calls this bread "daily." Why is that important? Why not pray for "weekly" bread or "monthly" bread?

_____

_____

_____

_____

_____

Have you ever really gone hungry or fasted?
What was that like?

_____

_____

_____

_____

_____

_____

_____

GO TO WAR

All day today, thank God for every meal or snack you eat, liquid you sip, and every piece of clothing you put on. How did that change your day?

BASIC TRAINING

CHAPTER 32
"FORGIVE US AS WE FORGIVE"

If we confess our sins, He is faithful and righteous to forgive us our sins and to cleanse us from all unrighteousness.
—1 John 1:9

Good news! God is willing to forgive you.

He is faithful (you can trust Him) and just (it's done righteously and legally) to forgive your sin. That act of forgiveness, paid for by Jesus Christ, cleanses-purifies-wipes clean our record of sin.

Now that you're forgiven, can you forgive others? Jesus said you'd better.

"For if you forgive others their wrongdoing, your heavenly Father will forgive you as well. But if you don't forgive people, your Father will not forgive your wrongdoing."
—Matthew 6:14–15

Then Peter came to Him and said, "Lord, how many times could my brother sin against me and I forgive him? As many as seven times?" "I tell you not as many as seven," Jesus said to him, "but 70 times seven."—Matthew 18:21–22

"And if he sins against you seven times in a day, and comes back to you seven times, saying, 'I repent,' you must forgive him."—Luke 17:4

So . . . if I'm holding some grudge against someone . . . If I still hate someone . . . If I cannot get to the place of total forgiveness . . . God will not forgive me?

It's like the Parable of the Unforgiving Servant.

READ MATTHEW 18:21–35

The servant knew he was forgiven and yet he did what?

_____

_____

_____

_____

Was the master's punishment fair?

_____

_____

_____

The servant showed no signs of forgiveness to anyone in his life, even though he was totally forgiven. Is that servant us?

Jesus stated in these verses some pretty difficult challenges. He said if we forgive, God will forgive us. Wait, is forgiveness conditional? Isn't forgiveness freely given to all who ask for it? Yes, but . . .

Jesus addressed the heart of the forgiven saying, "If you forgive, then you understand forgiveness. If you hold back forgiveness, then your own forgiveness comes into question." The proof that we understand forgiveness and have been forgiven is revealed in our willingness to forgive others.

Then Jesus told His followers to forgive and to keep on forgiving. Peter wanted a limit on the forgiveness meter. Jesus said there was none. Some questioned how many times we could forgive repeat offenders.

Certainly at some point we can stop forgiving and say they've crossed the point of no return. Jesus said there's no such limit to our forgiveness so we should not place limits on others.

When we refuse to forgive, we are being prideful. We may feel powerful or justified in our anger. They hurt us, so we'll get them back by not forgiving. But this puts us on the seat of judgment rather than God and dishonors His right to judge all. In the end, we only punish ourselves with the pain and poison of bitterness.

Forgiving honors God and is best for everyone involved and shows that we truly understand forgiveness and are demonstrating the mercy and kindness of God to others.

GO TO WAR

Make a list of people you need to forgive. Don't give up your prayer time until you are convinced they are forgiven. Don't just say "I forgive." Make sure you no longer hold anything against them. Turn all judgment over to God, and let Him handle it all. Understand that if God can forgive them, you can too. No sin is unforgivable.

I need to forgive:

_____

_____

_____

_____

_____

_____

_____

_____

_____

_____

_____

_____

_____

_____

BASIC TRAINING

CHAPTER 33
"DO NOT BRING US INTO TEMPTATION"

No temptation has overtaken you except what is common to humanity. God is faithful, and He will not allow you to be tempted beyond what you are able, but with the temptation He will also provide a way of escape so that you are able to bear it.—1 Corinthians 10:13

What are your biggest temptations?

_____

_____

_____

_____

_____

_____

When you succumb to those temptations, how do you feel?

_____

_____

_____

_____

_____

_____

_____

God does not lead us into temptation. He does not want us to sin. Satan leads us into temptation. He wants us to sin.

In Genesis 3, Satan tempted Adam and Eve to sin by doing three things.

- Verse 1: "Did God really say . . ." Satan created DOUBT about God's Word. He can't disprove it, so he just questions it.

- Verse 4: "You will not die . . ." Satan flat out LIED about God's Word.

- Verse 5: "God knows when you eat your eyes will be open . . ." Satan created MISTRUST between God and man.

Temptations are based upon doubts, lies, and mistrust. The defense against these temptations, or the "way out of them" as stated in 1 Corinthians 10:13, is knowing God's Word and believing it to be true. If we protect our minds with truth, Satan can't sneak in and twist things around, making you think you deserve to do something or find a way to justify your sin.

So we pray for God to show us the way out of temptation, to prevent Satan from tempting us.

We also need to know that temptations are not sin. Temptations are invitations to sin by Satan. When a thought comes to your mind, you then have the choice to accept the invitation or reject it. Even by mulling over the temptation for a while and seriously considering it, you can sin in your mind.

Jesus received these invitations, three of them, while fasting in the wilderness. Jesus denied each request immediately and pushed back with His knowledge of Scripture.

Truth is the best defense against temptation (doubts, lies, and mistrust). We need to understand more truth to receive more protection from sin.

GO TO WAR

Here's a list of temptations. Recognize which areas you are weakest in and ask God for strength to fight against the sin.

- **Porn/sex**

- **Drugs/drinking**

- **Pride/selfishness**

- Lying/cheating/stealing

- Rebellion/disobedience

- Ungratefulness/complaining

- Anger/bitterness

- Food/eating

- Power/wealth

- Laziness/procrastination

- Hate/revenge

- Entertainment/fun

- Negativity/divisiveness

- Gossip/meanness

- Other: _____

_____

_____

_____

_____

_____

_____

BASIC TRAINING

CHAPTER 34
"DELIVER US FROM THE EVIL ONE"

"I have given them Your word. The world hated them because they are not of the world, as I am not of the world. I am not praying that You take them out of the world but that You protect them from the evil one. They are not of the world, as I am not of the world."—John 17:14–16

When Jesus prayed for His followers, as recorded in John 17, He prayed for their protection from the evil one. As long as good tries to dwell in an evil world, Christ's followers will always be under attack.

Jesus said to His father some important truths about us that we need to remember:

- We have the Word of God. Truth defends against the world's desires.

- We are not of the world, but we must remain in the world if there is any hope for the world.

- Jesus is the best model for living in the world, showing us how to be IN but not OF the world.

As long as we live in the world, we must pray for God's protection, to save us from hurt and harm.

Missionaries especially put themselves in dangerous situations overseas. Satan wants pastors and Christians to fall morally to cause believers to mistrust the church. Many families exist in harmful environments with unstable people.

We must pray that God saves them from harm.

The Lord is my rock, my fortress, and my deliverer, my God, my mountain where I take refuge, my shield, and the horn of my salvation, my stronghold.—Psalm 18:2

We must pray for God to be our shield, our defense, our wall, our rock, our army. We must run to Him for protection.

We cannot get lazy or think that Satan won't harm us. We are vulnerable if we stand up for good and proclaim God's name in our lives. Anytime you take a stance for God, Satan will try to get you to fall.

GO TO WAR

Think of vulnerable areas in your life where you need protection. Is it a certain individual that you fear? Are there situations where you need support? Think of God as a rock, fortress, deliverer, mountain, refuge, shield, horn, and stronghold around you next time.

BASIC TRAINING

CHAPTER 35
THE MODEL PRAYER

So as you wrap up Basic Training, Jesus gave us some step-by-step thoughts on what a prayer should include.

Praying is not a formula or a script to read. Remember, praying is all about relationship. What if you called your dad on the phone every Sunday and said,

"My father who lives in Toledo, how awesome is your name. Your work is great. You always get it done, at work and at home. Send me today some daily groceries and forgive me of my wrongdoings and I promise I'll forgive others too. Please help me not to be tempted and save me from harm. Bye!" And you hung up.

You did this for years and years. Would you have a relationship with your dad? No. You said things to him but you didn't really talk to him or express to him uniquely how you felt.

The same holds true for a prayer to God. By following the model, your prayer could go something like this . . .

My heavenly Father, who loves us all and desires a relationship with all His children . . . you who sit in heaven on His throne, a place of authority, awaiting us as we will one day come to be with You in our eternal home.

You are so holy. All Your thoughts are holy. All Your decisions are holy. All You say is holy. I want to be more like that. I want this world to be more holy.

Please do things to bring Your kingdom rule to us here on earth. Please let Your will, Your plans and pleasure guide our lives. Help me to do my part by being obedient. By Your grace, I can help advance Your kingdom here.

I know You will provide for me today. You always provide. Whatever I need, it will be there, because You love to give. Thank You for everything I have.

And please forgive me of all of my sins. Help me not to do stupid and foolish things today. Help me not to disappoint You. As You forgive me, I should forgive others. They too will try to hurt me, but if You don't hold things against me, I won't hold things against them.

Keep me away from anything that tempts me. Divert my eyes. Redirect my attention. I don't want to be tempted and fail.

Save me from evil and the intentions of Satan. I want to glorify You in everything I do. I am Yours. Amen

The next day, another prayer. It can be different and fresh. The order changes, but the elements Jesus outlined are important to remember.

- **God is your Father**

- **He is in heaven**

- **He is holy**

- **His kingdom and desires will be done**

- **He rules over earth and heaven**

- **He provides**

- **He forgives (and we should too)**

- **He helps us defend against temptations**

- **He saves us and protects us**

GO TO WAR

Remember those ten prayers? Rewrite them keeping in mind what you've learned so far in Basic Training.

1. _____

2. _____

3. _____

4. _____

5. _____

6. _____

7. _____

8. _____

9. _____

10. _____

ADVANCED TRAINING

ADVANCED TRAINING

CHAPTER 36
WILL GOD GIVE ME WHATEVER I WANT WHEN I PRAY?

As we move up in the ranks of a prayer warrior, we all have hard questions. Sure we have faith, but these issues keep rattling around inside of us. Doubt? Confusion? Maybe. There are answers to these tough questions to give you advanced training in your prayer life.

We wonder about prayer when we read verses like these:

"Keep asking, and it will be given to you. Keep searching, and you will find. Keep knocking, and the door will be opened to you."—Matthew 7:7

"And if you believe, you will receive whatever you ask for in prayer."—Matthew 21:22

"Therefore I tell you, all the things you pray and ask for—believe that you have received them, and you will have them."—Mark 11:24

"Whatever you ask in My name, I will do it so that the Father may be glorified in the Son. If you ask Me anything in My name, I will do it."—John 14:13–14

What do these verses mean to you as you read them?

_____

_____

_____

_____

_____

_____

_____

_____

_____

_____

_____

I can get whatever I want if I just ask for it! What a dangerous way to think. Sounds more like a spoiled brat. Jesus said those statements not to tell us He's a genie in a bottle. He wanted us to know He's open and available to hear what's on our heart.

Sure, we can ASK God but we can't EXPECT God to give us everything we want. He will give us things we need. He will give us the good things we ask for. He will give us things that advance His kingdom and honor His name.

And if we're a follower of Jesus Christ, then we should only ask for what Jesus wants, as indicated by John 14:13–14 "in My name" (more on that later).

How do we know what Jesus wants? We know His will because we read His Word, walk closely with Him in all we do, and obey His commands. We know His promises and His heart.

If God wants it, He'll get it. If we agree with what God wants, then we'll get what we want too.

God is not an open catalog, taking orders from us. We have to be careful that we are not demanding in our prayer life. ASK, SEEK, and KNOCK only on the doors God leads you to.

If we pray God's will, we will see more prayers answered than ever before. If we walk closely with Him and delight in Him, then He will give us the good desires of our hearts (John 15:7; Psalm 37:4). We'll be more satisfied with our prayer life as we see more prayers answered.

GO TO WAR

Think about what you want (especially those ten prayers you've been focusing on). What is it you want? Then think about what God wants. Are they the same?

ADVANCED TRAINING

CHAPTER 37
HOW DO I KNOW GOD'S WILL?

Pay careful attention, then, to how you walk—not as unwise people but as wise—making the most of the time, because the days are evil.—Ephesians 5:15–16

Obviously you can't ask for anything you want and God gives it to you. Sometimes what we want right now is not what we want later. Sometimes what we want may be based upon a sinful desire and is not God's best.

God wants you to want what He wants.

If you pray for what God wants, you'll get what you want because God wants it too.

Here's a quick list of things that God wants according to the Bible:

- That no one should die and all should repent (2 Peter 3:9)

- To wipe away all tears and take away all pain (Revelation 21:4)

- That all should be forgiven (Acts 10:42–43)

- To take the gospel into the world (Matthew 28:18–19)

- To be with us always (Matthew 28:20)

- For people to receive the Holy Spirit (John 14:26)

- To be convicted because of our sins (John 16:8–11)

- To read the Bible (Romans 15:4)

- To love one another (John 13:34–35)

- To exhibit the fruit of the spirit (Galatians 5:22–23)

- To gather His children together (Matthew 23:37)

- For sinners to repent (Luke 15:3–7)

- For us to go to church (Hebrews 10:25)

- To be salt and light (Matthew 5:13–16)

And on and on and on and on . . .

Read 1 John 5:14–15, and answer these questions.

If you pray God's will, does that guarantee it will happen?

YES   **NO**

If you pray God's will, does that mean it will happen right away?

YES   **NO**

What stands in the way of God's will?

PEOPLE'S WILL

It comes down to God's will versus a person's will. God respects our free will and allows us to make choices. He doesn't want robots doing whatever He programs us to do. He wants us to love Him by decision, not coercion.

As for other areas of your life, God knows the best path and He makes it clear what you should do. For example:

- What college to choose?

- Whom to date/marry?

- Where to live/roommates?

- What college major to pick?

- What career to choose?

Many choices are between good, better, and best. It's not like all colleges are evil and only one is good. Or working as a cashier or working as a nanny are diametrically opposed. The important thing is to surrender yourself to the Lord and make choices with His will in mind, not yourself.

Here's a good method to discovering the right choice:

"But seek first the kingdom of God and His righteousness, and all these things will be provided for you."
—Matthew 6:33

What path keeps you most involved in God's kingdom?

What path is best to live out His righteousness?

He'll put the rest together for you if that's His will.

GO TO WAR

Pray today for God's will. Desire only His will. Remove your will from the equation, meaning don't consciously map out a result in your head but remain open to God's resolution.

ADVANCED TRAINING

CHAPTER 38
DO I HAVE TO BE RIGHTEOUS FOR GOD TO HEAR MY PRAYERS?

Is anyone among you suffering? He should pray. Is anyone cheerful? He should sing praises. Is anyone among you sick? He should call for the elders of the church, and they should pray over him after anointing him with olive oil in the name of the Lord. The prayer of faith will save the sick person, and the Lord will restore him to health; if he has committed sins, he will be forgiven. Therefore, confess your sins to one another and pray for one another, so that you may be healed. The urgent request of a righteous person is very powerful in its effect. Elijah was a man with a nature like ours; yet he prayed earnestly that it would not rain, and for three years and six months it did not rain on the land. Then he prayed again, and the sky gave rain and the land produced its fruit. —James 5:13–18

In order for your prayers to be heard, do you have to be "righteous"? Do you have to be on the level of an elder in the church or a great prophet like Elijah? James raises the bar when he says the prayer of righteous person is powerful and effective. Read 1 Peter 3:10–12.

We want our prayers to be powerful and effective but do we have to be righteous for that to happen? Righteousness is to be right with God through Jesus and to be walking rightly before Him and others.

What do you think when you read this verse?

"Be perfect, therefore, as your heavenly Father is perfect."
—*Matthew 5:48*

_____

_____

_____

_____

_____

_____

Perfect? Absolutely perfect? Without any flaws? Impossible. But a worthy goal.

If God's goal for us was GOODNESS . . . what would that mean? We can interpret that all kinds of ways. "I'm a good person." "I'm good to people." "I do good to others." *Good* is a loose term that can be defined many different ways.

PERFECTION . . . we all understand—to live completely without any sin. This word *perfect* can also mean to be completely mature in Christ, lacking nothing (James 1:4; Colossians 1:28).

God wants you to be perfect like He is perfect, but the world doesn't. God knows you live in a sinful world, surrounded by sinful choices, in a body predisposed to sin. He knows being perfect is absolutely impossible apart from His grace and Christ's righteousness. We all sin and fall short.

God is calling us to grow up in Him and to live a righteous life. Righteousness puts us on the path of the goal of perfection.

RIGHTEOUS means being in a right relationship with God. If your prayers are going to be effective, you have to be "right" with God. Which means:

- **You've submitted your will to His.**

- **You're listening to God speak to you.**

- **You're reading about God's will in His Word.**

- **You're applying those principles to your life daily.**

- **You're striving daily to be more like Christ.**

You may not be perfect, but you should be striving for maturity and spiritual completion. That's what God looks for.

James says Elijah was a sinful person like us ("a nature like ours") and yet he accomplished great things. His prayers could stop rain and start them again. We should strive to be like Elijah, a prophet completely sold-out to God who dedicated his whole life to spreading God's message.

If God only heard the prayers of totally perfect, sin-free people, He wouldn't hear very many. Yes, He hears the prayers of imperfect people, but the ones who are most righteous, most in line with God's will, see more prayer success in their lives because they want what God wants, stay clean and close, and live as God wants them to live.

GO TO WAR

Pray to live a righteous life. Ask God to show you areas that need fixing, like a leaky pipe, where righteousness is draining out of your life. Repair those leaks with confession and repentance so righteousness can flow through you uninterrupted.

ADVANCED TRAINING

CHAPTER 39
IF I WORRY, WILL I RUIN MY PRAYER?

We read this verse and we start to worry . . .

Don't worry about anything, but in everything, through prayer and petition with thanksgiving, let your requests be made known to God. And the peace of God, which surpasses every thought, will guard your hearts and minds in Christ Jesus.
—Philippians 4:6–7

Even though the verse tells us not to worry, we might worry that we are worrying. Some believe that because they worry they are not a Christian. Others wonder if worry is a sin.

Are you a worrier?

YES   **NO**

Are you worried that you lied and gave the wrong answer above?

YES   **NO**

There are different kinds of worry.

"I hope everyone is okay"—This kind of worry shows reasonable concern.

"Everybody could die!"—This kind of worry shows unreasonable expectations.

Worry and concern are very different. Here is when worry is a problem.

- **If you constantly dwell on the situation in your mind (preoccupation).**

- **If you are assuming the worst rather hoping that God will bring about His best.**

- **If you consider all kinds of possibilities—realistic and unrealistic —and believe that they will all happen (false expectations).**

PREOCCUPATION and FALSE EXPECTATIONS smother our faith because they refuse to hand over the result to God.

A person believes that their WORRY will help to bring about a solution. Thinking about something over and over will not bring about the desired result.

PREOCCUPATION tells God that YOU must be involved in the situation and that YOU don't trust God to handle it.

FALSE EXPECTATIONS tell God that He can't handle the situation and life/Satan/the world will win in the end.

The Bible indirectly calls worry a sin because Jesus repeatedly commanded us not to worry about even one thing.

How? Worry shows a lack of trust in God. By constantly dwelling and rethinking all the possibilities, you are saying that God cannot handle this situation. Complete trust releases the problem to God.

Praying releases the problem and outcome into God's hands. It is the antidote for anxiety. It's the way to effectively hand over the situation to God.

God, this issue is huge, but I trust You are working on it and that whatever happens will be the best for all of us right now. Period. Done. Released.

Any other thoughts after that point do absolutely nothing to affect the outcome.

"Can any of you add a cubit to his height by worrying? If then you're not able to do even a little thing, why worry about the rest?"—Luke 12:25–26

Jesus joked in this statement by saying no short person grew taller by worrying. *"Oh Lord, why am I only four foot eight? Why aren't I taller?"*

He also said, *"If you're a weak person and got yourself into this mess, why do you think you can worry and get yourself out of it?"* Worrying indicates the belief that you have the power to change the situation better than God—that you know better.

Our prayer time should be a time of release. We should walk away from the situation more calmly, at ease because we've handed all our issues over to God and we're trusting that He's going to work.

Breathe. Relax. God's got this.

GO TO WAR

What areas of your life do you tend to worry about the most? Ask yourself why you can't let go? Confess to God that you don't trust Him. See those issues in His hands, on His agenda, entered into His schedule. Know He has full control and sees the problem from all sides.

ADVANCED TRAINING

CHAPTER 40

WHY MUST I WAIT SO LONG FOR GOD TO ANSWER PRAYER?

Be silent before the Lord and wait expectantly for Him.
—Psalm 37:7

When we pray about a job, we want to hear the "ding" of our e-mail indicator telling us an employer has accepted our application.

When we pray about a relationship, we want the phone to "ring" with that person on the other end apologizing to us and asking for forgiveness.

When we need money, we want to hear the "knock" at the door as a mysterious delivery person drives away leaving an envelope of cash.

But it rarely works that way. God sometimes answers right away, but most of the time we must be patient.

Sometimes we have to wait . . . and wait . . . and wait . . .

Waiting is normal. People in the Bible waited all the time.

- Abraham waited until he was ONE HUNDRED to have his son Isaac.

- Jacob worked FOURTEEN YEARS to get the wife of his dreams.

- Moses waited through TEN PLAGUES until his people were let go.

- The Israelites waited FORTY YEARS to get to the Promised Land (their own fault).

- Jesus waited THIRTY YEARS until He announced to the world who He was and why He was on earth.

If they had to wait, then we have to wait. WHY?

If all prayers were answered instantaneously, how would that affect us?

_____

_____

_____

_____

_____

_____

_____

_____

_____

Wouldn't we become prideful and demanding if we got what we wanted the minute we asked for it?

Waiting is the laboratory of faith. It tests us and develops us into patient people.

Waiting tests our trust in God. Think of all the pieces God has to move into order to secure our prayer request. We believe that He's doing what He can to make it all fall into place.

Waiting causes us to examine our hearts. We ask ourselves if our will is truly God's will. We confess sin during that time. Our hearts grow more compassionate.

Waiting creates expectation. If you don't expect anything to happen, then you doubt. If you expect God to be working and the answer to be coming (today, tomorrow, in two weeks, or two years), you'll be more excited about the outcome.

Waiting produces increased praise. If we've waited a long time for a result, we rejoice greatly when it comes. The amount of the wait multiplies the degree of joy when a prayer is answered.

What should you do while you wait? Thank God He is using this WAIT to . . .

- **DEVELOP** your faith

- **INCREASE** your trust

- **EXAMINE** your heart

- **CREATE** more excitement

- **PRODUCE** greater praise

GO TO WAR

What are you waiting for? Say these verses while you wait and know God is working.

At daybreak, LORD, You hear my voice; at daybreak I plead my case to You and watch expectantly.—Psalm 5:3

Wait for the LORD; be strong and courageous. Wait for the LORD.
—Psalm 27:14

We wait for Yahweh; He is our help and shield.—Psalm 33:20

Be silent before the LORD and wait expectantly for Him; do not be agitated by one who prospers in his way, by the man who carries out evil plans.—Psalm 37:7

I put my hope in You, LORD; You will answer, LORD my God.
—Psalm 38:15

I waited patiently for the LORD; and He turned to me and heard my cry for help.—Psalm 40:1

LORD, look! They set an ambush for me. Powerful men attack me, but not because of any sin or rebellion of mine.—Psalm 59:3

LORD, I hope for Your salvation and carry out Your commands.
—Psalm 119:166

I wait for Yahweh; I wait and put my hope in His word.
—Psalm 130:5

I wait for the Lord more than watchmen for the morning—
more than watchmen for the morning.—Psalm 130:6

ADVANCED TRAINING

CHAPTER 41
DO I HAVE TO PRAY "IN JESUS' NAME"?

In the book of Acts, we see the power of Jesus' name. CIRCLE the words that indicate the name of Jesus.

"Repent," Peter said to them, "and be baptized, each of you, in the name of Jesus Christ for the forgiveness of your sins, and you will receive the gift of the Holy Spirit."—Acts 2:38

But Peter said, "I don't have silver or gold, but what I have, I give you: In the name of Jesus Christ the Nazarene, get up and walk!"—Acts 3:6

"By faith in His name, His name has made this man strong whom you see and know. So the faith that comes through Him has given him this perfect health in front of all of you." —Acts 3:16

So they called for them and ordered them not to preach or teach at all in the name of Jesus.—Acts 4:18

Barnabas, however, took him and brought him to the apostles and explained to them how Saul had seen the Lord on the road and that He had talked to him, and how in Damascus he had spoken boldly in the name of Jesus.—Acts 9:27

And he commanded them to be baptized in the name of Jesus Christ. Then they asked him to stay for a few days.—Acts 10:48

And she did this for many days. But Paul was greatly aggravated, and turning to the spirit, said, "I command you in the name of Jesus Christ to come out of her!" And it came out right away.—Acts 16:18

This became known to everyone who lived in Ephesus, both Jews and Greeks. Then fear fell on all of them, and the name of the Lord Jesus was magnified.—Acts 19:17

Then Paul replied, "What are you doing, weeping and breaking my heart? For I am ready not only to be bound but also to die in Jerusalem for the name of the Lord Jesus."—Acts 21:13

The name of Jesus means the authority of Jesus. When we use those words, we are saying we are doing something because we understand the passion and purpose of Jesus Christ. We are accomplishing what He wants us to do.

Ambassadors are sent to the furthest reaches of the world in the name of that country. They carry with them the government's power and represent the best interests of the nation.

As Christians, we go into all the world representing Jesus Christ. We are serving and speaking in the name of Jesus—based upon His authority, not ours, His righteousness, not ours, and what He has done, not what we have done.

So when we pray and say "In Jesus' name" we are saying by His authority, doing what it is He wants us to do. It should not be spoken lightly or routinely.

The name carries responsibility and power.

The phrase indicates under whose authority you place yourself, so you should be praying as one who is under the authority and name of Jesus Christ.

GO TO WAR

Before you pray "In Jesus' name," make sure you are praying for the will of God. If you are praying as a representative of Jesus Christ, then use the phrase. If not, then you are using His name in vain.

Do not misuse the name of the Lord your God, because the Lord will not leave anyone unpunished who misuses His name.—Exodus 20:7

ADVANCED TRAINING

CHAPTER 42
DO I HAVE TO CLOSE MY EYES, KNEEL, BOW MY HEAD, FOLD MY HANDS, AND SAY "AMEN" WHEN I PRAY?

RIGHT NOW: Kneel, bow, fold your hands, and close your eyes.

What does this position express to you? Why would it be helpful when you pray?

_____

_____

_____

_____

_____

_____

_____

Daniel kneeled when he prayed.

When Daniel learned that the document had been signed, he went into his house. The windows in its upper room opened toward Jerusalem, and three times a day he got down on his knees, prayed, and gave thanks to his God, just as he had done before.—Daniel 6:10

When praying, the closing of eyes and bowing of head represent humility. If a king walked into the room, the servants diverted their eyes, feeling unworthy to make eye contact with royalty. You are saying, when you close your eyes and bow your head, that you have entered the presence of the King of kings.

The folding of hands and the bowing of knees represent surrender. If a hand is folded into another hand, it is empty of any weapons and ready for service. Kneeling down, a person cannot run away quickly but he must remain in position until told he could move.

These positions should represent the heart of the one praying. Humility and surrender.

You don't have to put your body into that position unless it reminds your heart to be in that position. If kneeling helps you to be more humble, go for it.

Closing of eyes is usually a good tactic because it shuts out distractions. When you close your eyes, you can picture the conversation between you and God better. While it has its advantages, it's not necessary to close your eyes for God to hear you (especially if you drive and pray). But it may help you hear God better.

"I do not call you slaves anymore, because a slave doesn't know what his master is doing. I have called you friends, because I have made known to you everything I have heard from my Father."—John 15:15

Remember, Jesus calls us a friend, not just a servant.

But do remember this. Bowing is the common position in heaven.

For this reason God highly exalted Him and gave Him the name that is above every name, so that at the name of Jesus every knee should bow—of those who are in heaven and on earth and under the earth—and every tongue should confess that Jesus Christ is Lord, to the glory of God the Father.
—Philippians 2:9–11

Bowing is totally acceptable there, so why not here?

Amen has become the sort of PERIOD at the end of the prayer. It socially works because it tells people "I'm done praying, so you can lift your head."

But the word AMEN is more than that. The word means TRUTH, FAITH, SO BE IT, LET IT BE SO.

We say it as a stamp to what we just prayed, like the politician who says at the end of a commercial, "I approve this message."

But since prayer is communication and our communication with God should never stop, we don't have to end our transmission to God like we're talking to Him on walkie-talkies. "Over and out."

You can use AMEN any time you want. Someone says some truth that you agree with. AMEN. Someone expresses a desire that you feel God approves. AMEN. You hear a sermon that lifts your spirit. AMEN. The word doesn't just end prayers; it emphasizes and agrees with truth. Amen?

GO TO WAR

If you don't normally bow, kneel, and fold your hands when you pray, do so and see if that helps your prayer time. Did it help you humble your heart?

SNIPER SCHOOL

SNIPERS are about precision, focusing in on a specific target.

That's how we must pray.

Many of us pray SHOTGUN prayers—spiritual blasts that we hope hit their target.

Snipers require effort and concentration. They have a purpose and a target.

Shotguns blast away, hoping someone will be affected, not really knowing who or how.

If you shotgun pray that someone will get saved at your school and a kid in your chemistry class comes to youth group, hears the gospel, and dedicates his life to Christ . . . that's a good thing, right? But can you look back and definitely say your prayer made the difference?

Not as much as if you prayed specifically for that kid in your chemistry class to come to youth group and hear the gospel.

God can work with either prayer. However, He wants you to truly experience the wonder and power of prayer when you specifically focus on one target.

How do you pray?

LIKE A SNIPER   ## LIKE A SHOTGUN

To pray with sniper-like skill, you will need to change the focus of your prayers, looking through a sight and not firing from the hip.

Let's look at how to pray SPECIFICALLY, STRATEGICALLY, AND STRENUOUSLY.

Keep in mind a sniper is under orders. He is told by his superiors what to do and who the targets are. He cannot operate under his own assumptions.

As you pray specifically, don't let your desires take over. If you do, you will be disappointed, believing prayer doesn't work.

Prayer does work. It doesn't work when you pray your will.

A sniper has a specific purpose in the overall plan. He's not the ground troops. He sees the bigger picture from a certain vantage point.

Prayer is part of the overall strategy. Others will work on the ground and affect the outcome. Prayer focuses on the bigger picture but sees a specific target.

Snipers must wait long hours for the targets to show up. It's hard work.

Specific targeted prayers take time also. Require patience. Distractions can sneak in. Apathy too. Stay on mission! Don't give up.

As a SNIPER . . .

PRAY GOD'S WILL. . . . . *Not your desire.*

PRAY WITH PURPOSE. . . . . *See the big picture.*

PRAY WITH PERSEVERANCE. . . . . . *Don't give up.*

Let's use this skill to pray for some specific areas —Family, School, College, Future Spouse, Career, Friends, Country.

SNIPER SCHOOL

CHAPTER 43
YOUR FAMILY

PRAY SPECIFICALLY FOR YOUR FAMILY

Your family has a major influence on you. Mom, Dad, brothers, sisters. They have their own struggles in their lives. Let's focus on them.

SHOTGUN: How would you generally pray for your family?

_____

_____

_____

_____

_____

_____

_____

Now think more specifically.

FOCUS: What influence is pressuring your family?

_____

_____

_____

FOCUS: Who needs the most prayer?

_____

_____

_____

FOCUS: What do you feel God wants to do in their life?

_____

_____

_____

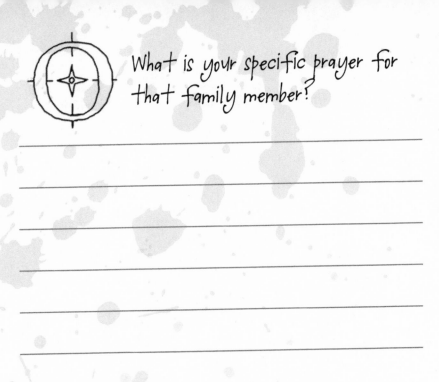

What is your specific prayer for that family member?

_____

_____

_____

_____

_____

PRAY STRATEGICALLY FOR YOUR FAMILY

What do you think is your involvement in this prayer?

_____

_____

_____

_____

_____

Whose involvement in this prayer can make a difference?

_____

_____

_____

_____

Whose involvement would surprise you?

_____

_____

_____

What sorts of resources are needed?

_____

_____

_____

_____

_____

What is God's purpose for that family member?

_____

_____

_____

_____

_____

_____

What is God's strategic will for your family?

_____

_____

_____

_____

_____

_____

PRAY STRENUOUSLY FOR YOUR FAMILY

So many factors can be discouraging. You are up against some pretty tough forces. Don't give up.

When did you start praying for your family?

DATE: ___/___/_____

What setbacks did you encounter?

DATE: ___/___/_____

DATE: ___/___/_____

DATE: ___/___/_____

DATE: ___/___/_____

DATE: ___/___/_____

What progress did you see?

DATE: ___/___/_____

DATE: ___/___/_____

DATE: ___/___/_____

DATE: ___/___/_____

DATE: ___/___/_____

When do you feel the prayer was specifically answered?

DATE: / /

What factors did you specifically, strategically, strenuously pray for that you saw occur?

_____

_____

_____

_____

_____

_____

_____

_____

_____

_____

_____

SNIPER SCHOOL

CHAPTER 44
YOUR SCHOOL

PRAY SPECIFICALLY FOR SCHOOL

Let's focus on your school. Remember, this is your prayer that you feel God wants you to pray for your school, the administrators, teachers, leaders, sports, events, and students.

SHOTGUN: How would you generally pray for your school?

_____

_____

_____

_____

_____

_____

Now think more specifically.

FOCUS: What do you think is God's will for the specific timing of that prayer?

_____

_____

_____

_____

_____

FOCUS: Who do you think specifically is a part of God's will for that prayer?

_____

_____

_____

_____

_____

FOCUS: How do you think specifically God wants that prayer to happen?

_____

_____

_____

_____

_____

_____

_____

FOCUS: What other specific factors do you think need to be addressed?

_____

_____

_____

_____

_____

_____

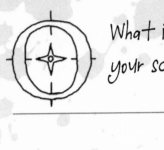

What is your specific prayer for your school?

_____

_____

_____

_____

_____

PRAY STRATEGICALLY FOR SCHOOL

What do you think is your involvement in this prayer?

_____

_____

_____

_____

_____

Whose involvement in this prayer can make a difference?

_____

_____

_____

Whose involvement would surprise you?

_____

_____

_____

What sorts of resources are needed?

_____

_____

_____

_____

_____

_____

What is God's purpose behind this prayer?

_____

_____

_____

_____

_____

_____

_____

What is God's strategic will for
your school?

_____

_____

_____

_____

_____

PRAY STRENUOUSLY FOR SCHOOL

So many factors can be discouraging. You are up against some pretty tough forces. Don't give up.

When did you start praying for your school?

DATE: ___/___/_____

What setbacks did you encounter?

DATE: ___/___/_____

DATE: ___/___/_____

DATE: ___/___/_____

DATE: ___/___/_____

DATE: ___/___/_____

What progress did you see?

DATE: ___/___/_____

DATE: ___/___/_____

DATE: ___/___/_____

DATE: ___/___/_____

DATE: ___/___/_____

When do you feel the prayer was specifically answered?

DATE: ___ / ___ / _____

What factors did you specifically, strategically, strenuously pray for that you saw occur?

_____

_____

_____

_____

_____

_____

_____

_____

_____

_____

_____

SNIPER SCHOOL

CHAPTER 45
YOUR COLLEGE

PRAY SPECIFICALLY FOR COLLEGE

If you're in high school, you're probably thinking about college or a trade school. It's time to start praying so God can get you at the right place according to His will.

SHOTGUN: How would you generally pray for your future education, college, training, or seminary?

_____

_____

_____

_____

_____

_____

Now think more specifically.

FOCUS: What will be your major?

_____

_____

_____

_____

FOCUS: Who will be your roommate?

_____

_____

FOCUS: Do you need to be in-state or out-of-state?

_____

_____

FOCUS: Do you have the money to further your education?

_____

_____

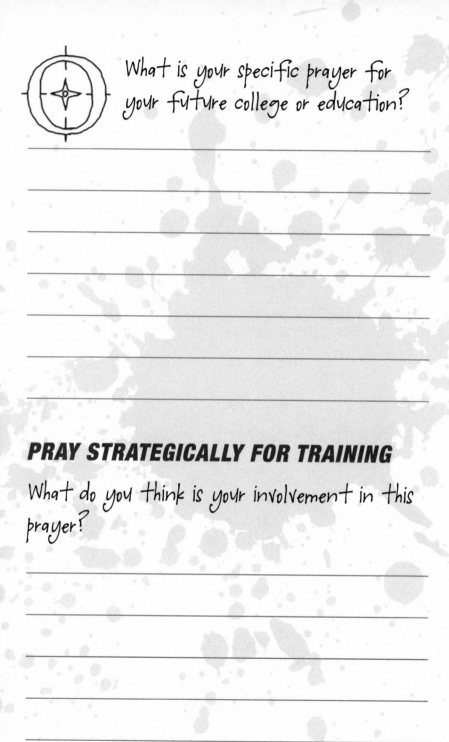

What is your specific prayer for your future college or education?

_____

_____

_____

_____

_____

_____

PRAY STRATEGICALLY FOR TRAINING

What do you think is your involvement in this prayer?

_____

_____

_____

_____

_____

Whose involvement in this prayer can make a difference?

_____

_____

_____

Whose involvement would surprise you?

_____

_____

_____

What sorts of resources are needed?

_____

_____

_____

_____

_____

_____

_____

What is God's purpose behind you going to school in the future?

_____

_____

_____

_____

_____

_____

What is God's strategic will for your future schooling?

_____

_____

_____

_____

PRAY STRENUOUSLY FOR COLLEGE/ TRAINING

So many factors can be discouraging. You are up against some pretty tough forces. Don't give up.

When did you start praying for your education?

DATE: / /

What setbacks did you encounter?

DATE: / /

DATE: / /

DATE: / /

DATE: / /

What progress did you see?

DATE: / /

DATE: / /

DATE: / /

DATE: / /

DATE: / /

When do you feel the prayer was specifically answered?

DATE: ___ / ___ / _____

What factors did you specifically, strategically, strenuously pray for that you saw occur?

_____

_____

_____

_____

_____

_____

_____

_____

_____

_____

_____

SNIPER SCHOOL

CHAPTER 46
YOUR FUTURE SPOUSE

PRAY SPECIFICALLY FOR A FUTURE SPOUSE

Down the road, maybe you're thinking about getting married. If you are going to get married, right now that spouse is already on the earth. Maybe you've met. Maybe not. That spouse is experiencing things that could affect the two of you later. It's never too early to start praying for that person.

SHOTGUN: How would you generally pray for your future spouse?

_____

_____

_____

_____

_____

_____

_____

Now think more specifically.

FOCUS: What qualities about that person are "must haves"?

_____

_____

_____

_____

FOCUS: What qualities about that person are deal breakers?

_____

_____

_____

_____

FOCUS: How will you know that person is right for you?

_____

_____

_____

_____

_____

_____

What is your specific prayer for your future spouse?

_____

_____

_____

_____

PRAY STRATEGICALLY FOR A FUTURE SPOUSE

What do you think is your involvement in this prayer?

_____

_____

_____

_____

Whose involvement in this prayer can make a difference?

_____

_____

_____

Whose involvement would surprise you?

_____

_____

_____

What sorts of resources are needed?

_____

_____

_____

_____

_____

_____

What is God's purpose behind you meeting, dating, and marrying this person?

_____

_____

_____

_____

_____

_____

What is God's strategic will for your future spouse?

_____

_____

_____

_____

_____

PRAY STRENUOUSLY FOR A FUTURE SPOUSE

So many factors can be discouraging. You are up against some pretty tough forces. Don't give up.

When did you start praying for your future spouse?

DATE: / /

What setbacks did you encounter?

DATE: / /

DATE: / /

DATE: / /

DATE: / /

DATE: / /

What progress did you see?

DATE: / /

DATE: / /

DATE: / /

DATE: / /

When do you feel the prayer was specifically answered?

DATE: ___/___/___

What factors did you specifically, strategically, strenuously pray for that you saw occur?

_____

_____

_____

_____

_____

_____

_____

_____

_____

_____

_____

_____

SNIPER SCHOOL

CHAPTER 47
YOUR CAREER

PRAY SPECIFICALLY FOR YOUR CAREER

A job makes money for a period of time. A career is a path driven by passion and purpose. We want to make sure we have the right career for us where God can use us. We want to wake up in the morning and look forward to our career. Whether it is working from home, serving in ministry, or working at another company, we want God's very best.

SHOTGUN: How would you generally pray for your career?

_____

_____

_____

_____

_____

_____

Now think more specifically.

FOCUS: What things interest you?

_____

_____

_____

_____

FOCUS: What are you passionate about?

_____

_____

_____

_____

FOCUS: What careers always looked appealing?

_____

_____

_____

_____

 What is your specific prayer for your future career?

_____

_____

_____

_____

PRAY STRATEGICALLY FOR YOUR CAREER

What do you think is your involvement in this prayer?

_____

_____

_____

Whose involvement in this prayer can make a difference?

_____

_____

_____

Whose involvement would surprise you?

_____

_____

_____

What sorts of resources are needed?

_____

_____

_____

_____

What is God's purpose for your career?

_____

_____

_____

_____

_____

What is God's strategic will for your career?

_____

_____

_____

_____

PRAY STRENUOUSLY FOR A CAREER

So many factors can be discouraging. You are up against some pretty tough forces. Don't give up.

When did you start praying for your career?

DATE: ___/___/_____

What setbacks did you encounter?

DATE: ___/___/_____

DATE: ___/___/_____

DATE: ___/___/_____

DATE: ___/___/_____

DATE: ___/___/_____

What progress did you see?

DATE: ___/___/_____

DATE: ___/___/_____

DATE: ___/___/_____

DATE: ___/___/_____

When do you feel the prayer was specifically answered?

DATE: ___/___/_____

What factors did you specifically, strategically, strenuously pray for that you saw occur?

_____

_____

_____

_____

_____

_____

_____

SNIPER SCHOOL

CHAPTER 48
YOUR FRIEND

PRAY SPECIFICALLY FOR YOUR FRIEND

It's hard to watch a friend fall far from God. We want that person to fall in love with God and begin to surround themselves with positive friends and healthy habits.

SHOTGUN: How would you generally pray for your friend?

_____

_____

_____

_____

_____

_____

Now think more specifically.

FOCUS: What does God want for that friend's life?

_____

_____

_____

_____

FOCUS: What obstacles is that friend up against?

_____

_____

_____

_____

FOCUS: Who else could influence that friend?

_____

_____

_____

_____

What is your specific prayer for your friend?

_____

_____

_____

_____

PRAY STRATEGICALLY FOR YOUR FRIEND

What do you think is your involvement in this prayer?

_____

_____

_____

Whose involvement in this prayer can make a difference?

_____

_____

_____

Whose involvement would surprise you?

_____

_____

_____

What sorts of resources are needed?

_____

_____

_____

_____

What is God's purpose for your friend to find
God?

_____

_____

_____

_____

What is God's strategic will for your friend?

_____

_____

_____

_____

PRAY STRENUOUSLY FOR YOUR FRIEND

So many factors can be discouraging. You are up against some pretty tough forces. Don't give up.

When did you start praying for your friend?

DATE: ___ / ___ / _____

What setbacks did you encounter?

DATE: ___ / ___ / _____

DATE: ___ / ___ / _____

DATE: ___ / ___ / _____

DATE: ___ / ___ / _____

DATE: ___ / ___ / _____

What progress did you see?

DATE: ___ / ___ / _____

DATE: ___ / ___ / _____

DATE: ___ / ___ / _____

DATE: ___ / ___ / _____

When do you feel the prayer was specifically answered?

DATE: ___ / ___ / _____

What factors did you specifically, strategically, strenuously pray for that you saw occur?

_____

_____

_____

_____

_____

_____

_____

SNIPER SCHOOL

CHAPTER 49

YOUR COUNTRY

PRAY SPECIFICALLY FOR A COUNTRY

"God so loved the world . . ." He loves every ethnic group and every religious group. He wants them all to hear the truth.

SHOTGUN: How would you generally pray for the world?

_____

_____

_____

_____

_____

_____

_____

Now think more specifically.

FOCUS: What country has God put on your heart?

_____

FOCUS: Why would God put you in touch with that country?

_____

_____

FOCUS: Who else could influence that country?

_____

_____

What is your specific prayer for that country?

_____

_____

_____

PRAY STRATEGICALLY FOR A COUNTRY

What do you think is your involvement in this prayer?

_____

_____

_____

_____

_____

Whose involvement in this prayer can make a difference?

_____

_____

_____

Whose involvement would surprise you?

_____

_____

_____

What sorts of resources are needed?

_____

_____

_____

_____

What is God's purpose for this country to find God?

_____

_____

_____

_____

What is God's strategic will for this country?

_____

_____

_____

_____

PRAY STRENUOUSLY FOR A COUNTRY

So many factors can be discouraging. You are up against some pretty tough forces. Don't give up.

When did you start praying for that country?

DATE: ___ / ___ / _____

What setbacks did you encounter?

DATE: ___ / ___ / _____

DATE: ___ / ___ / _____

DATE: ___ / ___ / _____

DATE: ___ / ___ / _____

DATE: ___ / ___ / _____

What progress did you see?

DATE: ___ / ___ / _____

DATE: ___ / ___ / _____

DATE: ___ / ___ / _____

DATE: ___ / ___ / _____

When do you feel the prayer was specifically answered?

DATE: ___/___/___

What factors did you specifically, strategically, strenuously pray for that you saw occur?

_____

_____

_____

_____

_____

_____

_____

_____

_____

_____

_____

_____

THE
WAR
ROOM
JOURNAL

THE WAR ROOM JOURNAL

CHAPTER 50
GOING TO WAR

If God's army is going to make a difference in this fight, it starts with us. Let's read this very important verse to prepare us for battle.

If . . . My people who are called by My name humble themselves, pray, and seek My face and turn from their evil ways, then I will hear from heaven, forgive their sin, and heal their land.—2 Chronicles 7:13–14

IF MY PEOPLE . . .

Change in a community begins when GOD'S PEOPLE decide to make a difference.

It will take effort, commitment, and sacrifice.

It will not be inspired by blame and finger-pointing.

It will start when God's people take the initiative.

ARE YOU ONE OF GOD'S PEOPLE?

| YES | NO |

If you answered YES, then move on.

WHO ARE CALLED BY MY NAME . . .

Joining the ranks of God's people is a calling.

You are called by God to pray and to see a difference in the world around you.

It's voluntary, yes, but it's a calling too. God has you at a specific place, at a specific time, with a specific task. He calls you in as a specialist.

ARE YOU CALLED BY GOD?

YES   **NO**

If you answered YES, then move on.

WILL HUMBLE THEMSELVES . . .

Arrogant soldiers die on the battlefield.

They think they know best and push ahead of the Commander in Chief. They run out into the fight unprotected and without clear direction, feeling they can do it themselves. They "work alone."

God can only use humble soldiers who submit themselves fully to God and listen only to Him and not to their own desires.

ARE YOU A HUMBLE SOLDIER?

YES   **NO**

If you answered YES, then move on.

AND PRAY . . .

The task of the soldier is to pray.

It's a prayer war. That's the whole purpose of this book.

ARE YOU READY TO PRAY?

YES   **NO**

If you answered YES, then move on.

AND SEEK MY FACE . . .

When we pray, we seek the face of God. We want to make sure God's attention is focused on the area we are praying for. If God is facing away from the situation, meaning it's not on His agenda, we need to pray for a different thing.

When we look to someone's face we want to find their expression. Happy, sad, disappointed, angry . . . Seeking God's face is determining His attitude about a situation.

ARE YOU READY TO SEEK GOD'S FACE?

YES   **NO**

If you answered YES, then move on.

AND TURN FROM THEIR EVIL WAYS . . .

Evil soldiers cannot be used by God. They have not submitted their lives to the righteous training that's required. They are out of shape, weakened by sin, and fattened by worldly desires.

To be used in battle, you must confess your sins and repent. Repentance is not just saying YOU'RE SORRY for your sins, but committing to NEVER AGAIN engage in that sin ever again.

ARE YOU A SINNER?

YES   **NO**

CAN YOU REPENT OF YOUR SIN RIGHT NOW?
YES   **NO**

WILL YOU VOW TO NEVER AGAIN ENGAGE IN THAT SIN AGAIN?
YES   **NO**

If you answered YES to all the above, then move on.

GOOD NEWS!

You've vowed to do your part in the war; now God will do His part.

What will God do?

Hear. Forgive. Heal.

GOD WILL HEAR FROM HEAVEN

This is no minor task. Don't think, *Big deal, so God hears*. God hears the cry and recognizes the passion of His people.

God sits up and says, "Wow, they really want this. I'm going to do something spectacular."

When God knows that His people are on fire, it moves Him to action.

He hears and He steps in.

GOD WILL FORGIVE OUR SIN

God will forgive OUR sin. Through the acts of confessing, humbling, and submitting, God removes the guilt and stains from the lives of those who trust that Jesus paid the penalty for those sins.

In turn, they enter society as joyful, forgiven people. They begin forgiving people. Others see the love and return the love. They want to know where this love comes from.

They ask questions. They seek God. They find God.

GOD WILL HEAL THE LAND

As the people begin to experience God through God's people, healing occurs. People change. Churches change. Governments change. Laws change. Ideologies change. Philosophies transform. Agendas submit.

People—ALL PEOPLE—begin to call on God. Defenses drop. Weapons are destroyed.

A COMMUNITY, A SCHOOL, A STATE, A NATION, A LIFE IS TRANSFORMED!

So how did this all start?

GOD'S PEOPLE CALLED ON GOD—IN PRAYER AND IN CONFESSION.

Through the course of this book, you've learned what it means to be a prayer warrior.

But the battle is not over. It's just beginning.

As you continue to use *War Room Prayer Journal*, you will record your prayers on the day you proposed them to God, including the actual specific prayer, the specific answer, and the day the answer was given.

You will see purpose when you pray.

You will see progress when you pray.

You will see the power of prayer that you can look back on and be encouraged to pray more!

YOU HAVE YOUR ORDERS! TIME TO ENTER THE BATTLEFIELD.

WAR ROOM JOURNAL

Date	Prayer Request	Answer	Date Answered
		Yes No Wait	
		Yes No Wait	
		Yes No Wait	
		Yes No Wait	
		Yes No Wait	
		Yes No Wait	
		Yes No Wait	
		Yes No Wait	
		Yes No Wait	
		Yes No Wait	
		Yes No Wait	
		Yes No Wait	
		Yes No Wait	
		Yes No Wait	

Date	Prayer Request	Answer	Date Answered
		Yes No Wait	
		Yes No Wait	
		Yes No Wait	
		Yes No Wait	
		Yes No Wait	
		Yes No Wait	
		Yes No Wait	
		Yes No Wait	
		Yes No Wait	
		Yes No Wait	
		Yes No Wait	
		Yes No Wait	
		Yes No Wait	
		Yes No Wait	
		Yes No Wait	
		Yes No Wait	

Date	Prayer Request	Answer	Date Answered
		Yes No Wait	
		Yes No Wait	
		Yes No Wait	
		Yes No Wait	
		Yes No Wait	
		Yes No Wait	
		Yes No Wait	
		Yes No Wait	
		Yes No Wait	
		Yes No Wait	
		Yes No Wait	
		Yes No Wait	
		Yes No Wait	
		Yes No Wait	
		Yes No Wait	
		Yes No Wait	

Date	Prayer Request	Answer	Date Answered
		Yes No Wait	
		Yes No Wait	
		Yes No Wait	
		Yes No Wait	
		Yes No Wait	
		Yes No Wait	
		Yes No Wait	
		Yes No Wait	
		Yes No Wait	
		Yes No Wait	
		Yes No Wait	
		Yes No Wait	
		Yes No Wait	
		Yes No Wait	
		Yes No Wait	
		Yes No Wait	

Date	Prayer Request	Answer	Date Answered
		Yes No Wait	
		Yes No Wait	
		Yes No Wait	
		Yes No Wait	
		Yes No Wait	
		Yes No Wait	
		Yes No Wait	
		Yes No Wait	
		Yes No Wait	
		Yes No Wait	
		Yes No Wait	
		Yes No Wait	
		Yes No Wait	
		Yes No Wait	
		Yes No Wait	

APPENDIX A: YOUR STORY

Do you have a story? We all have a story about how we got here to this place, writing in a journal, committing ourselves to pray.

But about THE story. The story of your salvation.

How did that happen?

_____

_____

_____

_____

_____

_____

_____

_____

_____

_____

_____

_____

_____

Who was most important in your salvation
(besides Jesus)?

_____

_____

_____

_____

What does your salvation mean to you?

_____

_____

_____

_____

_____

_____

_____

_____

_____

APPENDIX B: THANK YOU, GOD!

In case you ever need a list of things to remember what God has provided for you or given you, refer to this page. DOG-EAR IT, for easy access when you pray.

_____

_____

_____

_____

_____

_____

_____

_____

_____

_____

_____

_____

FROM THE CREATORS OF **FIREPROOF** AND **COURAGEOUS**

WAR ROOM

PRAYER IS A POWERFUL WEAPON

Check out these previous films from the creators of **WAR ROOM**

WARROOMTHEMOVIE.COM | PROVIDENTFILMS.ORG

© 2015 AFFIRM Films & Provident Films. All Rights Reserved.

PRAYER IS A POWERFUL WEAPON

Tony and Elizabeth Jordan have it all—great jobs, a beautiful daughter, and their dream house. But appearances can be deceiving. Their world is actually crumbling under the strain of a failing marriage. While Tony basks in his professional success and flirts with temptation, Elizabeth resigns herself to increasing bitterness. But their lives take an unexpected turn when Elizabeth meets her newest client, Miss Clara, an older, wise widow who challenges Elizabeth to start fighting *for* her family instead of against her husband.

BONUS FEATURES

Includes a reading group guide and a color insert with behind-the-scenes movie photos

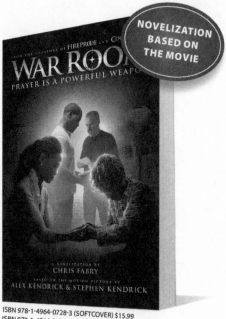

ISBN 978-1-4964-0728-3 (SOFTCOVER) $15.99
ISBN 978-1-4964-0729-0 (HARDCOVER) $22.99

www.WarRoomTheMovie.com
Read the book before you see the movie in theaters August 28, 2015!

www.tyndalefiction.com
© 2015 Faithstep Films, LLC. All rights reserved.
CP0941